K

KID NET

....
THE KID'S GUIDE
TO SURFING
THROUGH CYBERSPACE
....

Debra and Brad Schepp

HarperCollins*Publishers*

All of the photographs and illustrations in this book have been obtained from online sources, and have been included to demonstrate the variety of work that is available on the Net. The caption with each photograph or illustration identifies its online source.

HarperCollins books may be purchased for educational, business or sales promotional use. For information, please write: Special Markets Department, HarperCollins Publishers, Inc., 10 East 53rd Street, New York, NY 10022.

FIRST EDITION

Designed by Laura Lindgren

Library of Congress Cataloging-in-Publication Data
Schepp, Debra.
    Kidnet : the kid's guide to surfing through cyberspace / Debra and Brad Schepp. — 1st ed.
        p.   cm.
    Includes index.
    ISBN 0-06-273380-X (alk. paper)
    1. Computer networks. 2. Internet (Computer network)
3. Microcomputers. I. Schepp, Brad. II. Title.
TK5105.5.S333   1995
025.04—dc20   95-24444

---

95 96 97 98 99 ❖/RRD 10 9 8 7 6 5 4 3 2 1

To the memory of my paternal grandparents,
Jacob and Krainie Sorkowitz, who filled my youth
with love, wisdom, and happiness. Their lives
spanned a century. They saw incredible changes,
but they never would have believed this!
D.A.S.

To my paternal grandmother, Hortense Schepp,
whose strength and dignity I've always found inspiring.
B.J.S.

Selected Contents

Acknowledgments

Many people helped us gather the information we needed for this book. The online world is full of helpful, friendly people. It would not be possible for us to thank them each individually. We'll try to name a few who really went above and beyond.

On America Online, we'd like to thank Jerry Pectol of the Grandstand, Dan Skolnik, of ABC Rock & Road, and Henry Rosengarten of the Academic Assistance Center.

On CompuServe, a special thanks goes to Chuck Lynd of the Education Forum and Rilla Moulden of the YDrive. Also, thank you to Richard Warren, Richard and Susan Duncan, and Helen Jackson. Debra Young was also a big help, as usual.

On Prodigy we'd like to thank Barry Traver from the Homework Helper.

Helpful Webmasters and other online savants who gave freely of their time and who deserve a special thanks include:

Sandy Nicholson
Steve Bauman
Sandra Loosemore
Philip Greenspun
Andy Carvin
Deborah Ann Torres
Kevin Altis
Rob Hipschman
Bob Allison
Stephan Fitch
Gleason Sackman
David Newman
Jacqueline Hamilton
Diane Greer
Calvin J. Hamilton

Markus Kruse
Christopher McBride
Jeff Lewis
Brian Pinkerton
Isaac C. Dziga
Jill Lampi
Cathy Brandt
Doug Brooks
Greg Brooks
Mark Ahlness

A special big thank you to Linda Delzeit of Academy One and Dave Stanworth of the Games Domain. Also, a special thanks to Leona Williams for working with us on the profile of her husband, boxer Jake Williams. Bill Adler and Lisa Swayne of Adler & Robin books—you guys can take a bow. Thanks!

Thank you to Cynthia Barrett and Elissa Altman of HarperCollins Publishers. We are so pleased that they first thought this book was a good idea. We are also very grateful for their help in bringing our ideas into sharper focus.

Thanks to the people at Toshiba who let us borrow a Satellite T1960CT notebook computer. What a help!

And finally, to our children, Ethan and Steph. The online world is your future. Thank you for tolerating our distraction in the present while we write books.

Introduction

Because you live in the 1990s, you've been bombarded with news of the Information Highway. You can't pick up a newspaper or magazine or turn on the TV without hearing about "cyberspace." How much of this is real and how much of this is media hype? It can be very hard to know.

We've been exploring cyberspace for more than 10 years, so it's a little hard for us to feel the same hype that can overwhelm newcomers. We've also been parents for the same amount of time. That's why we've written this book for you. We feel qualified to help you sift through the hype and find the best of cyberspace to enjoy with your kids.

CONVENTIONS WE'VE USED IN THIS BOOK

As we've explored cyberspace, we've described for you exactly what we've found. You'll find that each description includes some common features.

NAVIGATION COMMANDS
Each description of an online offering includes the shortcut word users type in to move to that area. Using these commands is faster than using the services' menus, so they help you control your online costs a little. On the Internet, these shortcuts are anything but short! When you see (http://alphabet.soup), for example, you know that's the navigation command for a particular Web site.

PRICING SYMBOLS
We've also included symbols to indicate if the service is surcharged. For example, CompuServe and Prodigy surcharge some of their offerings. Next to the name of the offering, you'll find a (Plus). You may also find a ($)

symbol, which means the particular offering has a premium charge. We've included these symbols, because we wanted you have some warning whenever you were considering stopping off at a surcharged feature. If no symbol is listed, the service is part of the basic or core service offerings covered by your monthly subscription fee. You'll find complete pricing information about all of the services in Chapter 1.

PARENTAL GUIDANCE SYMBOL

When you see this symbol (T) next to a particular service description, you'll know that you should consider this area appropriate for your older kids, maybe your 13- and 14-year-olds. This is a difficult judgment call, because all parents have different opinions about what is appropriate for their kids and what is not. We're fairly strict about what our kids have access to in the media, and what you see here is based on our feelings about what we consider appropriate for our kids. Use this as a guideline, a little advice from other parents. Most of the service offerings are fine for everyone, but when you see this symbol, check it out for yourself before you take your 9- to 12-year-olds there.

THE DAWN OF A NEW WORLD

We parents are watching the birth of a new world; the world of cyberspace. Our kids will live in its maturity. Our children and their children, too, will look at us as pioneers who first charted the unknown territory they'll tame. They'll look at us with the same bemused tolerance that we use when we remember our grandparents with their first box-like car, or our parents with their first silly TV sets.

Make no mistake, the arrival of cyberspace into their lives will make our children's world vastly different from ours. After all, going into cyberspace allows us all to exist outside the realm of our physical beings. Our thoughts and essence travel out through our phone wires to meet with the thoughts and essences of countless others. No one knows what we look like. They only know the content of our thoughts and the way in which we express those thoughts.

This mind-to-mind communication breaks down many of the old barriers we humans have placed among us. It doesn't matter what color your skin is, which neighborhood you live in, or what type of car you drive. Eventually, it won't even matter which language you speak, because translation software will automatically convert messages from other languages into your native tongue. There has never before been such an opportunity for humans to live a truly global existence.

This mind-to-mind communication opens new doors of opportunity. In the spring of 1995, a young woman graduated from the University of Maryland at the main campus in College Park, MD. That is not newsworthy in itself, as countless young women have done the same. The fascinating news in this story was that this young woman stepped onto the campus for the first time on graduation day. She completed her entire four year college education from her home hundreds of miles away! She took courses and interacted with students and teachers online. Yet, when she hugged her professor in both greeting and farewell, they both felt they knew each other well.

Eventually our kids will sit in front of their TVs with their remote controls and travel through cyberspace at the push of a button. They'll access the world's information and people just as simply as they can now switch from cartoons to sitcoms. Traveling through cyberspace can already be more fun than watching TV, playing video games, and a special outing combined, because it's all of those things and more, all wrapped up in one bundle.

COME JOIN US

Before you go into cyberspace for real, let's take a sample trip online just to see what you might find. We'll pretend we have an hour to spend just wandering around. First let's stop into the Kids and Teens Student Forum on CompuServe. You can almost always find someone here to share a live chat. If we drop in during the afternoon, EST, we'll probably meet someone from England. Countless kids have told us that's when the phone rates are low in the United Kingdom, and their parents let them chat. Sure enough, there's Samantha with all of her 10-year-old charm. After catching up with Sam a bit, we remember that someone hasn't done his homework, and we're stumped with that math problem; blasted fractions!

Well, let's go online to America Online and stop by the Academic Assistance Center. In the live chat area, we find a teacher on duty. Unfortunately, she's a Spanish teacher and can't explain our math problem to us. But, don't fret, we'll page a math teacher with just the push of a few keystrokes. Okay, we've sent our request for help to the teacher page, now we can hang out for a few minutes to see if we can get some immediate help. While we're waiting let's go over to the Game Room, and see if they've added any new software games to download (transfer to our computer). Yep, sure enough there's a new version of our favorite shoot 'em up. We grab a blank disk, push a few buttons, now we have something fun to do when that homework is done! Here's a message from our teacher page. Our question has been sent to the right person, and we should be getting the help we need within the next few hours.

In the meantime, let's go back to CompuServe, because there's a live contest going on in the Dinosaur Forum. We'll get the chance to compete with other Dinokids and show off what we know about these great beasts. Also, we can get more information about this week's mystery dinosaur and decide which dinosaur we'll be when we do our dinosaur play-acting game later this week.

That was fun, but our hour's almost up. Let's connect to Prodigy and see what's new in Sports Illustrated for Kids. After catching up with the latest headlines and stats, we can save a little time for the Sports Illustrated Challenge. We're getting better at the trivia questions all the time! Now let's go see if the teacher on America Online has answered our question yet. Oh, yes, here it is, but too bad, she didn't solve the problem for us. She just explained the part we didn't understand and told us what to do next. Now we'll have to do that homework for ourselves after all. Well, let's get it done so we can play that new game we downloaded. Logging off, that's enough for today. Just think of everything we've done, and we never even got the time to go onto the Internet!

We told you going into cyberspace was fun! And, it gets to be more fun every day. It's evolving at lightning speed. You will see when you go online that between the time we wrote this book and today, there are new areas to visit and things to do. As just one example, America Online more than tripled its subscriber base between mid 1994 and mid 1995. The company, and all of its competitors, works hard to expand and continue to offer new and exciting things to these users. In the last year alone, all of the commercial online services began offering access to the Internet, and all of them have reduced the cost of using their services. We believe this trend will continue. Our goal, therefore, is to show you a sample of what's out there right now as we keyboard, and then give you the tools and confidence you'll need to fire up your rockets and start exploring!

GO ONLINE, LIVE OFFLINE

As you can see, we love going online. But, we promised to help you sift through the hype about cyberspace and find the best. We will work hard not to overstate this new world. Yes, it is a fascinating adventure. It's filled with opportunities for friendship, learning, exploration, and fun, but, so is the old real world. We'd like to show you and your kids how you can go online to enhance your enjoyment of your life here in the real offline world.

Yes, you can go online and find hundreds of people passionately devoted to soccer, but that won't take the place of running through the grass after the ball. Take what you find online, and bring it home. Share ideas and exchange thoughts in cyberspace, but then bring the best of that into the real world and get involved here. By all means, find interesting projects to help you work to improve the environment. But don't just read about them online; bring them home, and put them to work in your neighborhood. Cyberspace is an active, vibrant, ever-changing world. Harness it, and let it make your life richer and fuller.

HOW TO FIND US ONLINE

We hope you enjoy traveling through cyberspace and find our advice helpful. We'd love to hear from you. We're very curious to see what you think of the places we've described and to learn how you and your kids are using your online time. You'll find us at the following online addresses:

America Online: brads87901
CompuServe: 74777,137
Prodigy: GUFY38A
Internet Address: 74777.137@compuserve.com
Have fun and happy cybersurfing!

Welcome
to Cyberspace

When you were a child did you ever dream of having an all-knowing answer machine? You could ask it any question, and it would deliver the answer. It would never grow weary of the endless questions your eager and curious young mind generated. Or, maybe your fantasy was for a magic travel machine. You'd wake up in the morning and decide what today's destination would be. Should you explore the Arctic this morning and the rainforest this afternoon, or vice versa?

Childhood is a time for such fantasies, and never has there been a better time to turn your child's fantasy for travel, learning, and adventure into reality. It only takes a trip through cyberspace to make it happen. What exactly is cyberspace, how do you get there, and what will you find when you arrive?

Now, that depends on who you're asking. The practical answer is that cyberspace is a collection of commercial online services and the Internet. Online services are operated by companies that sell access

Figure 1.1 Downloaded via Internet from sunsite.unc.edu

to services, information, and software stored on their computers. The Internet is a worldwide conglomeration of millions of interconnected computers.

You can compare the Internet to public television, in that it's largely non-commercial (although that's changing) and its roots are in the government. The "commercial" services such as CompuServe, Prodigy, and America Online, then can be compared to NBC, CBS, and ABC. Just as public television and the networks are all part of the television medium, the Internet and the commercial services are all part of cyberspace.

But, ask individual cybernauts what cyberspace is, and you'll hear fantastic tales of fabulous destinations, steadfast friends, problems solved, answers received, and opportunities enjoyed. You'll learn about people from opposite sides of the earth working together on science projects. You'll hear stories about ongoing games played by scores of people scattered all over the globe. You'll have people tell you about chatting live with their favorite TV star or musician. You see, all of this is true, too.

So, in a sense, cyberspace is a product of both scientific reality and science fantasy. Yes, we humans could never have ventured into this new realm without the technology that makes modern computer communications what it is. But, now that we've arrived, we bring to cyberspace that ineffable quality that is human. We use cyberspace to reach out to each other and communicate. Cyberspace takes the computer and turns it right back to the humans who run it. Your kids will spend time in cyberspace, because that's where their peers will be.

WHAT EQUIPMENT IS NEEDED FOR CYBERSPACE TRAVEL?

To go online, you need four things: a computer, a modem, communications software, and a telephone line. It doesn't matter much what type of computer you have. The newer, faster, more powerful computers will make going online more fun, but if you have an older, slower computer you can still make the trip. The modem is the piece of hardware that allows your computer to send and receive information over your telephone line. Without a modem, your computer is incapable of communicating with remote computers. Communications software controls the operation of the modem. This software has only grown more powerful, less expensive, and easier to use over the years. You'll find more detailed descriptions of the different types of communications software in the next chapter. The final piece of equipment necessary is the one that most of us have, the telephone line. You can use your regular phone line for communicating via your computer. While you're online, callers to your phone will receive a busy signal.

For a detailed discussion of the hardware and software you'll use to go into cyberspace, please see Chapter 2. You'll also find some recommendations there about what we think is the best type of equipment to use and where you can get this equipment.

HOW MUCH WILL THIS TRIP COST?

Online travel is not cheap. See below for complete pricing information about each service.

COMMERCIAL ONLINE SERVICES PRICING INFORMATION

As with everything else, the price of using online services is subject to change. Please use the directions we include in the descriptions below to check current pricing when you log on to the service of your choice. All of the prices listed below are for the United States. International rates will vary.

AMERICA ONLINE

America Online uses a very easy pricing structure. As of this writing, a monthly subscription of $9.95 buys the user 5 hours of online time. Every hour after that is billed at a rate of $2.95 per hour. Unlike the other services, this monthly fee allows you access to everything in the service, with the exception of some third-party gateway offerings. These services use America Online as a gateway. An example of such a service that you'll find interesting is the Scholastic Network. The additional monthly fee for this service is not an America Online fee, but rather the cost of accessing Scholastic Network itself. All third-party gateways that carry additional charges are clearly marked. The only additional charge you'll incur that is generated by America Online itself is the fee for sending a paper copy or a fax of an email message.

To be sure this information is still current, enter the keyword (BILLING).

COMPUSERVE

We told you that the online world is an ever-changing one, and it's true. Just as this book was going to press, we received word from CompuServe that they were completely revamping their pricing structure. The good news is that CompuServe is now less expensive. The bad news is that this change came so close to press time that it was very difficult for us to incorporate all of the pricing changes throughout this book.

Under CompuServe's old pricing plan, the service was divided into Basic offerings, Extended offerings, and Premium offerings. Basic offerings were included with the monthly subscription fee. Extended offerings were charged at rates beginning at $4.80 per hour. Premium offerings carried additional charges, often established by the company providing the information through CompuServe.

In September 1995, this all changed. CompuServe eliminated the distinction between Basic and Extended services. Nearly 90 percent of CompuServe's service offerings are now included as basic elements of the service. Premium charges still apply to some research areas of CompuServe, but these generally carry surcharges on any online service they occupy. CompuServe clearly marks these areas for you.

CompuServe is now among the most competitively priced online services. You can still choose the standard monthly membership fee of $9.95, but this fee now includes five hours of access time. Additional time is billed at $2.95 per hour.

CompuServe also offers a super value club for its more active members. These members pay $24.95 in monthly membership fees and receive 20 hours of online time per month. Additional hours under this plan are billed at $1.95 per hour.

New members do not pay the monthly membership fee for their first month online. They also receive ten free hours for exploring the service.

We've gone to the book and made the changes that we could make to reflect these new prices. You may find references to "basic service offerings." These are now outdated, as mostly everything on CompuServe is "basic." You'll also notice screenshots from CompuServe may sometimes show "extended service charges." We could not change these so please disregard the reference to the extra charge. In a few cases, we have discussed services that carry premium charges. The information available to us at press time suggested that these still apply.

For up-to-the-minute pricing information, GO (RATES).

PRODIGY

Prodigy users can choose between two pricing options. The Basic Plan costs $9.95 and includes five hours of use for Prodigy's Core services. Each additional hour costs $2.95, and so do the Plus features.

Prodigy's Value Plan costs $14.95 and includes unlimited use of the Core services. It also includes five free hours of Plus service use. Each hour of Plus service use beyond the five costs $2.95.

For people planning to make heavy use of the Internet

via Prodigy there is a 30/30 Pricing Plan. This plan gives you 30 hours of monthly Prodigy access including the Internet for $29.95. Beyond 30 hours, the charge is $2.95 per hour.

For online billing information, use the Online Billing Information pull down screen from the Help heading. From here you can review current and past statements and check out the latest fees and charges.

DELPHI
Delphi offers new users five free hours to try out the service. When the trial period is over, members can choose between two plans.

The 10/4 plan costs $10 per month and includes 4 hours of use. Each additional hour costs $4.

The 20/20 Advantage Plan costs $20 per month and includes 20 hours of use. Additional hours cost $1.80. There is also a one-time entry fee of $19 for this plan.

EWORLD
Subscribers to eWorld receive 4 hours of time online for the monthly fee of $8.95. Each additional hour is billed at a rate of $2.95 per hour.

GENIE
At the time of this writing, GEnie warned that pricing updates were imminent. If you're interested in using the service, please check current rates by entering the Go word (RATES).

GEnie's monthly subscription fee costs $8.95 and includes up to 4 hours of connect time. The hourly rate beyond these 4 hours is $3. There is a prime time surcharge of $2 in addition to the $3/hour charge for time spent on GEnie between the hours of 8 A.M. and 6 P.M. local time. In addition, there is a $6/hour surcharge for modem speeds above 9600 bps. The 9600 bps surcharge is waived when using SprintNet or an "800" service.

IMAGINATION NETWORK
The ImagiNation Network has a large variety of pricing options from which to choose. No matter which one you

choose, remember that the rate for weekday use of the service between the hours of 7 A.M. and 6 P.M. is $6 per hour no matter which plan you've chosen. Discounted hours apply only for evening and weekends.

Details for the discounted plans are as follows:

Plan	Includes/Price	Additional Time/hour
Welcome Plan	5 hours for $9.95	$2.95
10 Plan	10 hours for $19.95	$2.75
15 Plan	15 hours for $29.95	$2.50
25 Plan	25 hours for $49.95	$2.25
50 Plan	50 hours for $99.95	$1.95

We'll give you some advice for controlling your costs in Chapter 4, but let's put the fees into perspective. Suppose your kids spend $20 per month online. That means they use all of the hours allotted to them by their monthly service charge, plus a few more. That $20 is the equivalent of ordering two pizzas a month for your family or taking the crew through a fast food drive-in about one and a half times. The cost of two premium cable TV channels would equal the same amount. So, yes, going online is an expense, and we don't want to minimize what that means to your family. On the other hand, going online brings worlds of information and opportunity into your home. It's interactive, so paying this money won't result in watching your kids zone out passively to the TV, and, unlike pizza and fast food, it contains no cholesterol!

THE COMMERCIAL ONLINE SERVICES

On the following pages we've described some of the online destinations you'll find featured in this book. By now, nearly everyone has heard of "The Big Three"; America Online, CompuServe, and Prodigy. We'll also introduce you to some lesser known services.

America Online

America Online (AOL) has worked hard to become an easy-to-use, consumer-oriented online service that's fun and easy for families to use. The company has worked hard to develop relationships with magazines such as Time Magazine, SPIN, Bicycling Magazine, and National Geographic to make popular print products available online.

AOL has also given away hundreds of thousands of copies of its software through magazines and mailings. Its goal was to saturate the market of new computer owners. The company has gone out of its way to make it easy for inexperienced computer users to hop online and start exploring.

This has led to explosive growth within the last few years. In mid 1995, America Online had more than 3 million members. According to Steve Case, President and CEO of America Online, that brought the company "from a distant third place in the online market to the fastest growing service in the U.S., in just one year." Very rapid growth usually results in some growing pains, and America Online has seen its share of these. For example, sometimes it can be difficult to actually connect with the service, because the network is busy. America Online is well aware of the frustration this causes its users, and it is aggressively addressing problems caused by the service's rapid growth.

AOL may not have the in-depth research offerings of some of the other services, especially CompuServe, but it is simple to use. It offers a wonderful variety of entertaining services for families and kids, and, for now, there is no better way to start exploring the Internet than through America Online.

Strengths and Weaknesses

The simple-to-use software is America Online's greatest strength. It makes the service completely non-intimidating. The service has a lot of fun offerings designed for kids and their families.

On the downside, it takes extra time to retrieve

AOL's pretty graphics. The messages on the message boards don't scroll off, so when you go to read them, you may find 50,000 messages or more. This is a little unwieldy.

What's Ahead
America Online has developed its own network—AOLnet—for dialing into America Online (see Figure 1.2). AOLnet offers local phone numbers that you dial, through your modem, to reach America Online and the services and people it includes. When you set up AOL's software it will help you easily choose a number, whether it's through AOLnet or another network, for reaching AOL. In response to its rapid growth, America Online is promising easy, fast access to the service through this still-developing network. AOLnet should be widely available by the time you read this.

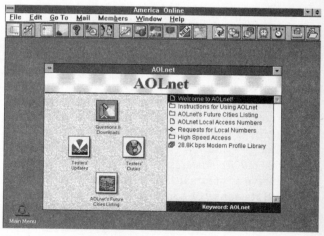

Figure 1.2 The AOLnet Screen on America Online

For customer service information contact:

America Online
8619 Westwood Center Drive
Vienna, VA 22182-2285
800.827.6364

CompuServe

CompuServe is the oldest and largest of the three major commercial services. It also has the greatest international membership. In mid 1995, CompuServe had more than 3 million users in the U.S. and 225,000 European members. It is famous for its business and computer-related services and for its impressive research tools such as Magazine Index, Knowledge Index, and Health Database Plus.

It comes to the family market later than its competitors, so as of this writing, you won't find as many offerings for kids. CompuServe is well aware of the huge market potential of this audience, and the company will expand its family offerings consistently in the future.

When you use CompuServe with your kids, you may not find as many flashy stops as you will on the company's two competitors, but what you do find is of extremely high quality. CompuServe's interface makes it easy to use, and CompuServe's users join together to form a "community" that is unsurpassed in the industry. Taking your kids onto CompuServe means taking them into a well-organized community, designed with safety in mind. Perhaps because CompuServe is the oldest service, you will meet people who have "lived" there a long time. They care about their online community the same way homeowners care about their neighborhoods.

Strengths and Weaknesses

CompuServe's greatest strengths are its research tools and its sense of community. Its weakness is its relative lack of service offerings for families and kids. This weakness will be addressed aggressively in the future. Also, although you can access the Internet through CompuServe, we feel AOL currently makes exploring the Internet easier.

What's Ahead

Early in 1995, CompuServe purchased Spry, the makers of Internet-in-a-Box. This $100 million purchase has helped CompuServe offer its users easy access to the Internet's hot World Wide Web (described later in this chapter). Ultimately this will be seamlessly integrated into CompuServe's service offerings. It will be transparent to the user whether he or she is on CompuServe itself or on the Internet.

CompuServe also announced the creation of a new animated online world called Worlds Away (see Figure 1.3). Worlds Away users will create their own animated personas, and these beings will inhabit animated places. Worlds Away users will be able to hold live chats, attend parties, conduct scavenger hunts, decorate their own apartments, and even run their own virtual businesses. While online, your animated person will occupy space; for example, a room where you can direct it to sit in the chair, handle the objects in the room, and share these objects with the other animated people you meet.

Figure 1.3 The Worlds Away Cafe as it will look on CompuServe

For customer service information contact:
CompuServe
5000 Arlington Centre Blvd.
P.O. Box 20212
Columbus, OH 43220
800.524.3388

Prodigy

Prodigy, owned by IBM and Sears, is in some ways the most commercial of the services covered here. Online ads, that appear at the bottom of your screen, have always been a part of Prodigy. A lot of people object to the ads, and in new versions of Prodigy they are supposed to become less intrusive.

By 1995, Prodigy had grown kind of stodgy, and while it offers many services of interest to parents and kids, how those services are presented leaves something to be desired. The graphics are cartoon-like, for example. Aside from the way Prodigy looks, it went through a period where it was not adding the type of interesting content that upstart AOL was, in particular. So Prodigy, while mass marketed by two of the biggest mass marketers in the world, became known as the station wagon of online services.

As we write this, in mid-1995, the prognosis for Prodigy is quite good. Early this year, Prodigy unveiled two key services: an integrated browser for accessing the World Wide Web (the first service to offer this), and Homework Helper, an ingenious service for kids that lets them easily access articles and pictures from hundreds of sources. Prodigy also announced that it would soon unveil a completely new, up-to-date interface later in 1995. It will be available by the time you read this.

Strengths and Weaknesses

Prodigy has the marketing and financial resources of IBM and Sears behind it. It offers a lot of interactive games, surveys, and quizzes that kids should like. It also offers more for little kids (e.g., Sesame Street) than the other services. Right now, its clunky interface, the ads, and the relative lack of games and other software for downloading are weaknesses.

What's Ahead

Prodigy's new interface (see Figure 1.4), based on early reports, will be a big improvement over its current interface. The ads should become less intrusive.

Kidnet

Also, Prodigy will fully integrate the Internet into its service at large. Users who are reading an article about the Rolling Stones, for example, will be able to click on an associated icon to move to the Stones' World Wide Web site. (This integration is something the other services will offer as well.)

For customer service information contact:
Prodigy Services Company
445 Hamilton Avenue
White Plains, NY 10601
800.PRODIGY

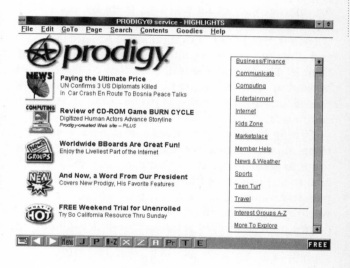

Figure 1.4 Prodigy's new Interface

THE INTERNET

The Internet is in a class by itself. As you may know, it is a product of the U.S. Defense Department. The Internet was established in 1969 as a way to ensure communication could get through in the event of a nuclear attack. (At least the computers could keep talking to one another.) From the beginning it was conceived as highly decentralized, which is its greatest strength and weakness. The Internet remained the province of the government and academia until fairly recently, when access was opened to the rest of us. While no one can say for sure just how many people use the Internet, estimates range from 3 to 32 million at this writing, with users in more than 100 countries.

Through electronic mail, Internet users can reach anyone using one of the commercial services. People using these other services can also reach Internet users. It's just a matter of addressing the message properly. For example, our CompuServe ID is 74777,137. An Internet user could reach us there by addressing the message to 74777.137@compuserve.com.

Face it, compared to CompuServe, America Online, and Prodigy, the Internet can seem like a lot of trouble. There's no central company to call to get hooked up. It's not owned by anyone; instead it's dispersed among hundreds of thousands of separate computers.

Getting hooked up to what's become a vast goldmine means making a decision or two about which route to take. It's worth the trouble. Your child will be able to see paintings from the Louvre, chat with keypals thousands of miles away, pose questions to the world's top authorities, and download and play games until their eyes grow bleary—this is all part of the Internet. Your child's potential for learning and fulfilling her curiosity at a whim is tremendous.

And the mountain's just building. The Internet will be a tool more indispensable than the telephone. The mother of all mediums. Better than TV, radio, the movies, you name it. Better, because it will offer everything those mediums offer—the information, the sounds, the video. The difference will be in the quantity and mix of what's available and how much control you have over "what's playing." Simply put, on the Net, you choose where you go and what you explore, whether it's a virtual trip to the Louvre, or a look at the school lunch menu at your child's school.

Bye Bye Barriers

At this moment, getting at all that good stuff can be frustrating. Connections are slow, so it can take a long time to get what you're after. There's also a lot of adult-type stuff on the Net that kids shouldn't see, and unlike the commercial services, the Internet has no central authority to help control access to such material. While you may also find suggestive photos, for example, on commercial services, the companies that operate them will help you control your child's access to such material.

Software's getting better, and as part of this better software, parents will be able to exercise more control over what their kids can check out on the Internet. Companies are developing this type of software now. Connections are also getting faster all the time. Soon you'll be able to access the Net at speeds hundreds of times faster than you can now. So, don't put it off, hop aboard!

THE WEB—WHAT'S HOT

The best part of the Internet—where all the action is—is the Web. The Web consists of more than 40,000 distinct sites, each with its own "home page." All kinds of institutions, companies, and even private individuals—from the Library of Congress to fans of Lego blocks—have set up Web sites. As soon as you're on the Net, you're only a keystroke or two away from the Web and all it has to offer.

The Web is popular because it makes the Internet manageable. It's brought order to chaos. Suddenly, getting what you want is a point and click process. Not only that, everything on the Web is linked. Click on a word that's highlighted, and you are automatically transported to a related Web site, or to a related topic that's part of the site you're "on." As the user, you may not even know whether that information comes from a computer based in the next town or on another continent.

For example, the Web's "White House Page" (shown in Figure 1.5) may refer to John F. Kennedy. Were you to click on Kennedy's name, your computer might pull up anything from an article on Kennedy, to a picture of Jackie and John together, to an entirely different Web site related to JFK. That could be anything from the Kennedy library site, to a site from someone interested in conspiracy theories concerning his assassination, to a college's repository of Kennedy-related artifacts.

Figure 1.5 The White House Web Page

Exploring the Web
There's a lot of junk on the Web that isn't worth your time or your child's right now. That's why throughout this book, at least as far as the Internet is concerned, we'll stress using "Best Of" and other good "pointer pages" to separate what's good from what's not. In these cases, someone has done the legwork for you, creating a launching pad from which you can readily explore services of interest. A good example is Uncle Bob's Kid's Page, described in Chapter 3. From this site, you can easily get to sites that "Uncle Bob" (Bob Allison) recommends. All you do is click on a high-

lighted word or phrase, such as Disney. The next thing you know, you've gone to the site you requested.

You can review sites like Uncle Bob's Kid's Page periodically yourself to see what's been added. You can then explore those pages that look interesting on your own. So, again, our goal is to point you to what's terrific right now, and teach you how to find other great stuff for yourself.

These reconnaissance missions serve two purposes. Obviously, you can pinpoint new sites for your child. But second, you become familiar with them yourself, and you stay current with the Internet. That will make it a lot more fun for you and your child when you cruise the Net together.

OTHER INTERNET LAUNCHING PADS

Throughout this book we'll be recommending interesting Internet newsgroups, files you can retrieve, and mailing lists your children may want to join.

Newsgroups
There are more than 10,000 Internet newsgroups. These are the Internet's equivalent to the message boards on CompuServe, Prodigy, and America Online.

Many of these newsgroups are, to use the movie industry's system, PG-, R-, and in some rare cases, X-rated. As the Internet is populated mostly by adults—a large percentage of whom are college students—the discussions are no-holds-barred. Anything goes—vile language, insults, you name it. (Sounds like life in a dorm.) So we'll recommend specific boards when we're able to locate kid-friendly ones. To locate other newsgroups use your software's search newsgroups feature and type in keywords of interest. Figure 1.6 shows you the Newsgroups screen on America Online.

Mailing Lists
Mailing lists are great if you want to receive a lot of email about a particular subject. Subscribers to a given

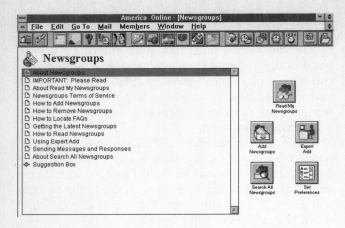

Figure 1.6 Accessing the Internet's Newsgroups through America Online

list share a common interest. They automatically receive articles and messages that are posted to the list. That's right, they're sent directly to their online mailbox, and at no charge. Some lists are managed by robot-like software (called Listserv) that can automatically add (subscribe) or delete (unsubscribe) you from the list—there's no direct contact with a human.

We've found that there are very few kid-oriented mailing lists for now, which may be a good thing because it's easy to oversubscribe and wind up with a flooded mail box. As with newsgroups, to locate mailing lists of interest, use your software's search mailing lists feature, or equivalent. Lists of mailing lists and newsgroups are also available through FTP (file transfer protocol) from various Internet archives. But we suggest that you keep these complete lists out of the reach of your young ones. Why give them the keys to the candy store?

FTP

This is the mechanism by which you retrieve files that reside on another computer and download them to your computer at home; a bit advanced for younger kids but your older kids will get the hang of it quickly.

Gopher

This is a menuing system which seeks to organize information and files that reside on a particular computer (a "gopher site"). Again, this can be a bit advanced for kids, but services such as America Online make using Gopher pretty simple. If a kid can point, click, read, and type he can retrieve files from a Gopher site.

SECOND-TIER SERVICES

These services may not currently have the huge user bases of the Big Three or the Internet, but their users are loyal.

Delphi

Delphi is currently a text-based service. You won't find slick or beautiful graphical interfaces when you log on, just menus. But, Delphi has been offering its users complete Internet access since 1992. The service is also very open to meeting the needs of its users. Many of the forums and special interest groups were not only suggested by Delphi members, but are now run by them as well.

Delphi is planning to launch a "graphical content-rich service," at this writing. As part of these expansion plans, the company announced it would open offices in New York and Boston, and hire 750 new employees. So keep your eyes on Delphi!

For customer service information contact:
1030 Massachusetts Avenue
Cambridge, MA 02138
617.491.3342

eWorld

In keeping with the philosophies of Apple Computer, its creator, eWorld is colorful, graphic, and lively.

Instead of the usual welcome screen, eWorld users
are greeted by a bright town center, complete with
buildings that represent different parts of the service
(see Figure 1.7). Click on the little post office to read
your mail, for example, or click on the little information booth for help. As you can imagine, this interface
will be very popular with kids.

Figure 1.7 eWorld Community Map

As of this writing, eWorld is only available to
users of Apple computers, but a Windows-based
version of the service is due out before the end of
1995. Also, eWorld has just announced a completely
new version of its service, dubbed Golden Gate. This
brings some exciting new features, such as "Speak."
Speak allows users to actually listen to online conferences by assigning different voices to conference
members. Not only that, users can do other things
in eWorld, while simultaneously listening to conferences.

For customer service information contact:
Apple Computer
20525 Mariani Avenue
Cupertino, CA 95014
800.775.4556

GEnie

Some claim GEnie's parent company, General Electric, has taken a laissez faire attitude toward GEnie. The old GEnie was conceived by GE as a way to make a little profit during off hours from the computers already in place for GE's email network. The company provided only a little money for the service's growth and development, so as you might guess, GEnie has fallen behind its competitors in these areas. GEnie is planning to offer its users Internet access near the end of 1995. It hopes to provide this access in a way that will be easier to use than its competitors.

For customer service information contact:
GEnie
401 N. Washington Street
VB-2
Rockville, MD 20850
800.638.9636

ImagiNation Network

Like the other online services, the ImagiNation Network's 55,000 members come online to make friends and hold live chats. But, the main purpose of the ImagiNation Network is to be an online amusement park. People log on to play games. They can play arcade-like games, board games, nearly every type of game you can imagine. The ImagiNation Network is crowded with kids who come here to play.

Before users log onto the ImagiNation Network, they use the software to create little icons of themselves. This face-making software is fun even if you never log onto the service! Add jewelry, hairstyles, and clothing to your image. When you log on, the other members of the service view you as the icon you've created.

Late in 1994, AT&T bought the ImagiNation Network. New software should be in place by now with enhanced sports games and educational games designed just for kids.

For customer service information contact:
The ImagiNation Network
577 Airport Blvd. #300
Burlingame, CA 94010
Voice: 800.462.4461
Fax: 415.548.0388

The Microsoft Network

As of this writing, Microsoft Corporation was working on the Microsoft Network to be unveiled as a feature of Microsoft's Windows 95 software. Windows users will be able to access the Microsoft Network directly from an icon on the Program Manager screen (see Figure 1.8), without loading any additional software. The company's plan is to make it as easy for Windows users to go online as it is for them to access their printers. The Microsoft Network will be graphical and colorful (see Figure 1.9), to make it inviting for the newcomer to the online world. Members will access Microsoft Network through a local phone call at speeds up to 14.4 bps.

Figure 1.8 Microsoft Network's icon scheduled to appear in Windows 95

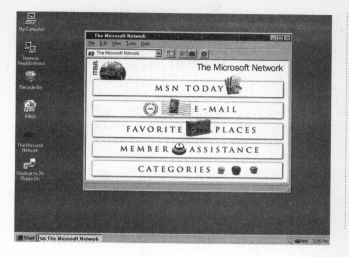

Figure 1.9 Microsoft Network's Opening Screen

By including the Network as part of its popular Windows 95 software, Microsoft assures itself of a wide audience from the outset. When the service is actually finished, it will be anything but "second tier." For now, we include it with the secondary services, simply because it wasn't publicly available at the time we wrote this book. Pre-release press information promises an exciting collection of online offerings.

The Network will offer areas for arts and entertainment, news and weather, and home and family to name just a few. Within these areas, you'll find some of the following highlights:

- Jazz Central Station: news releases, artists schedules, and historical backgrounds from the world of jazz.
- Collector's Direct Network: areas for hobbies and collectibles enthusiasts in 20 categories, including sports cards, comics, dolls, and coins.
- Martial Arts Network: martial arts enthusiasts will be able to chat with their peers, masters,

23

and grand masters about Tae Kwon Do, Karate, Aikido, Judo, and more.

- Best Friends Animal Sanctuary: an electronic gathering place for animal lovers, this is the online offering of the Best Friends Animal Sanctuary, the nation's largest sanctuary for abused and abandoned animals. It will include worldwide animal news, photos, videos, resource libraries, and "multimedia programming."
- Splash Kids Forum: a children's entertainment forum that will include an online magazine for kids and the Midas Valley Gold Rush adventure game, which will allow kids to roam around a simulated 3D world collecting clues to solve a mystery. A live chat and bulletin board will also be part of the service.

For customer service information contact:
Microsoft Corporation
One Microsoft Way
Redmond, WA 98052-6399
Voice: 206.882.8080
Fax: 206.93MSFAX

READY, SET, GO

By now you want to go online and start exploring. We recommend that you read the first four chapters of this book before you do. As you know, Chapter 1 gives you a feel for what this thing called cyberspace is all about. Chapter 2 will tell you exactly what you'll need in terms of hardware and software for going online. (Don't worry, we've been gentle with you, and you don't have to slip your pocket protector in place to get through it.) Chapter 3 will introduce you to some of your online neighbors, and you'll learn about the many options online users have for communicating with each other. Chapter 4 will give you some online rules for the road. You'll learn about netiquette, cost controls, and safety recommendations for traveling through cyberspace.

When you've finished reading these four chapters, start zipping around online according to your tastes and interests. In each of the subsequent chapters we've given you some of our own recommendations about what is fun and interesting. Of course, you'll find plenty of other things we didn't include, but that's part of the fun.

Building Your Spaceship

Relax. Getting online is hardly rocket science. If it were, Prodigy, CompuServe, America Online, and even the Internet would be a fraction of the size they are today. There are just not that many rocket scientists in the world! We mentioned earlier that getting online requires only four things: a computer, a modem, communications software, and a telephone line. (A mouse, while highly recommended, is not essential.) In this chapter we explore these four requirements.

BUYING A COMPUTER

We'll keep this short and to the point in case you already have your computer all set up with what you need. If you do, you may want to just skim this section for our basic recommendations.

IBM or Apple: What Should You Buy?
There are two basic flavors that computers come in: those made by Apple Computer or those made by

Figure 2.1 Downloaded via Internet from wuarchive.wustl.edu

26

IBM (or a manufacturer of IBM "clones"). Of the two, IBM computers are much more popular because they are generally less expensive, and there is more software available for them. Also, businesses have traditionally preferred them because they are conservative and like the idea of doing business with a strait-laced company such as IBM, rather than an avant garde trendsetter such as Apple. (Sorry, we couldn't resist.) We'll state right up front that we've used an IBM-compatible for more than ten years. We also own an Apple computer, however, and can appreciate the fine job Apple has done in making its computers easy to set up and use.

PCs or "IBM" Computers

Here are our recommendations for buying an IBM or compatible computer:

- Buy the "most" computer you can afford. There are many reasons for this, but the primary one is that multimedia software, including CD-ROMs such as Just Grandma and Me, require a lot of horsepower to run well. We're sure you'll want your kids to be able to use CD-ROM-based encyclopedias, as well as some of the new "edutainment" titles now available. As new software and CD-ROMs enter the market they will only require more and more in the way of memory, processor speed, hard disk space, etc.
- At a *minimum*, as of this writing, your computer should feature:

  A 486/DX2 microprocessor, operating at 66 megahertz.
  A super VGA monitor
  Twelve megabytes of RAM

Now it's quite possible to go online with a less expensive computer. And you can buy a used computer containing a 1980s-era microprocessor (a 286, for example) for a few hundred dollars. But we don't recommend it. For one thing, we are again assuming that as parents you will want to do more with your computer than just go online or word process documents. You'll want to go multimedia. And to do that you'll need a current model.

Even if your only aim is to go online, you'll want to be certain you can use a state-of-the-art modem to keep your time online and therefore your access charges to a minimum (when you are online you often are charged on a pay as you go basis; the longer the meter runs the more you pay). If you buy an older computer you may not be able to use it with a 28.8 bps modem. (More about modems in a minute.)

Where to Buy a PC

We like the mail order route. Prices are lower, and if you use the right vendor, technical support—at all hours—is just a phone call away. We've had good success with Dell, and surveys show the company's customer satisfaction levels are very high, so we're not alone.

Retailers, such as the computer superstores (e.g., CompUSA) are another popular option. However, you may not be able to get support when you need it. When you are first setting up a computer, especially a multimedia computer, there's nothing more important than that. A third option is the smaller, local computer retailer. If you buy your PC through a retailer, be sure to try to bargain for the best price. It is possible to do this.

Apple Computers

Apple Computer has done an excellent job of moving its computers into schools, so there's a good chance your child will be using one there. That may be reason enough to choose an Apple computer as your home computer.

Apple markets its Performa line of computers as "the family Macintosh"; this is the line Apple's tar-

Kidnet

28

geting toward parents of school-age students. Apple makes setting up a Performa simple. Everything you need comes in one box, including the color monitor, keyboard, mouse, and depending on the specific model chosen, a CD-ROM drive and modem, and as many as 23 software programs preinstalled. If you buy a Performa you can rest assured that the software your child uses on her Apple LC computer at school will be completely compatible with your new computer.

Performas currently range in price from $1,000 to $2,600. For the location of your nearest Apple retailer call 800.538.9696.

MODEMS

A modem is what brings the outside world of online services into your home. In short, it makes it so your computer can send and receive information over your telephone line. There are three basic types of modems: PC Cards (for laptop or notebook computers); internal modems, which fit inside your computer in an "expansion slot," and external modems, which connect to computers via a cable. We're going to assume that you will be setting up a desktop computer for home use and will therefore be shopping for an external or internal modem.

Stick with external modems. They are easier to set up; you just attach them to the outside of your computer through a serial port on the back. To install an internal modem you have to actually open up your computer, and then carefully insert it into an expansion slot. Most people would rather not bother with this. External modems are more portable than internal modems, and include lights so you can see when data is being sent or received. They are slightly more expensive than internal modems, but in this case the added convenience justifies the extra cost.

Aside from that, the most important thing about a modem is the speed at which it sends or receives data. We recommend you buy a modem that can send and receive data at 28,800 bits per second (commonly abbreviated as 28.8). As mentioned earlier, the longer you are online, the more you'll pay when accessing a service such as America Online. Even if there's a surcharge for using a faster modem (and these surcharges are disappearing), it's still worth it. Also, because you'll be using a modem with your kids—you know from experience that kids don't have a lot of patience—you'll appreciate that speed, especially when downloading large text files, sound files, or graphic files, which can be very large.

TIME/COST FOR
DOWNLOADING A 1 MEGABYTE FILE[1,2]

SPEED (BPS)	TIME (MINUTES)	COST[3]
2400	68	$3.40
9600	17	$0.85
14,400	10	$0.50
28,800	5	$0.25

[1]*Courtesy of US Robotics*
[2]*Assumes the file is uncompressed*
[3]*Based on an average cost of $3.00/hour*

As long as you're buying a modem anyway, get a data/fax modem. These receive faxes and can also send them if they're in electronic form. The data and fax speeds may differ. Again, the data speed should be 28.8 bps; make sure the fax speed is at least 9600 bps; 14,400 (or 14.4) is better. Not all modems are created equal. Look for a name brand such as Hayes or U.S. Robotics. By the time you read this you should be able to buy a 28.8 external modem for under $200.

COMMUNICATIONS SOFTWARE

Now that you have your computer and modem, you'll need software that controls the modem's operation. Prodigy, America Online, and eWorld require that you use communications software provided by them for access. That's just as well because these programs are easy to set up and use. CompuServe users can use the CompuServe Information Manager or a program such as NavCIS (both available from CompuServe). However, they can also use any commercially available communications program to access CompuServe (this same choice, commercial or company-supplied, also applies to Delphi and GEnie).

To access the Internet, you'll use the software provided by your Internet Service Provider (ISP), for example, a company such as PSInet/Pipeline. You can also use the same software you use to get onto Prodigy or one of the other commercial services—it all depends on the route you've chosen to get to the Internet.

It's likely that eventually you'll find you need a generic communications program. For example, if you want to access electronic bulletin boards or free-nets (described in Appendix B), you'll definitely need a generic communications program.

Your modem probably came with communication software. If you are a Windows user, you have a built-in program called Windows Terminal. This program may not be as easy to use as some others, but it has the obvious advantage of being "free." Programs that we've used and can recommend are Procomm Plus and HyperAccess on the IBM/DOS side. For Macintosh communications, White Knight and SitComm come highly recommended.

TELEPHONE LINES

We're willing to bet you have one of these already. Just one word of advice here: if you'll be online regularly, you may want to consider a second line just for this purpose. This has two advantages: your family will still be able to receive calls while you are online, and you'll still be able to make calls while you're online. This comes in very handy if you have to call an online services company for technical support. If you do not get a separate line (and we didn't for years), but have call waiting, be sure to disable call waiting while you are online. If you don't, incoming calls can knock you offline. Disabling call waiting can be handled through your communications software very easily, upon setup.

Your local telephone company will offer a service called ISDN, for Integrated Services Digital Network, if it does not do so already. Through ISDN you'll be able to send and receive data at 128,000 bps, which will make retrieving sound and graphics files much less time consuming. Right now, ISDN service is relatively expensive (about $25 per month, plus per-minute charges; special hardware is extra). But these costs should come down as competition in this area increases.

GETTING STARTED WITH THE MAJOR ONLINE SERVICES

Most commercial online services offer new users complete start-up kits that are easy to install and start using. Many services are also pleased to give new users a few hours of free trial time to explore their offerings. Use this free time to do some exploring as you choose your favorite corners of cyberspace.

Check Chapter 1 for its customer service contact information. Most services are glad to send you everything you need to get online.

HOW TO CONNECT TO THE INTERNET

The easiest way to connect to the Internet is through one of the major commercial online services. They all offer access to the Internet's newsgroups, mailing lists, files, and the World Wide Web. Prodigy was the first commercial service to offer this kind of access. (See Figure 2.2)

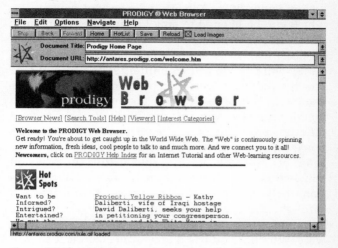

Figure 2.2 The Web Browser Screen from Prodigy

We suggest you sample the Internet through one of these services. They all make navigation simple; you'll have no additional software to buy; and you'll be able to try the Net as part of your initial free time offering.

If you then decide that the Internet is worthwhile (and we think you will) you may want to find another access route. Going through Prodigy, for example, is convenient, and there's something nice about being able to get to everything you're interested in online by going through just one service. You may pay extra for this convenience. Accessing Prodigy costs $9.95 per month for five hours of use; additional hours are billed at $2.95 per hour. A newly introduced 30/30 pricing plan gives Prodigy users 30 monthly hours of Internet access for just $30; additional hours are $2.95 each. Through Pipeline, one of the options discussed below, you can receive unlimited monthly

Internet access for only $35. (Your charge may vary depending on the network you use to dial in to the Internet.)

A second option is to go through an Internet Service Provider (ISP). ISPs are independent companies, which can be likened to small telephone companies. They provide a service—access to the Internet—for a monthly fee. For an average of $15 to $40 per month, an ISP will provide you with Internet access, and give you the software tools you need to get started. The trouble is, this software may take some tweaking to install correctly. And you are likely to need several different programs. If you want to check out an ISP, however, make sure they offer a SLIP (Serial Line Internet Protocol) or PPP (Point-to-Point-Protocol) connection (a PPP connection is best). SLIP connections help ordinary mortals connect to the Internet through special software and their own phone lines. PPP connections are similar but use different software. Whether you use a SLIP or PPP connection will depend primarily on what the provider offers.

Here are some other details you'll want to be sure about:

- The ISP provides Internet access via a local phone call from your location
- It provides telephone support
- The ISP can handle the speed of your modem (one last time: we recommend one that operates at 28.8 bps)

For a list of Internet Service Providers contact:
InterNIC Information Services
P.O. Box 85608
San Diego, CA 92186
619.455.4600

As you can tell, this option is for the more technically inclined.

We sometimes use the third option: a complete service provider. PSInet/Pipeline and Netcom (Net-

cruiser) are two of the most popular. These companies not only provide you with access to the Internet,
but they also give you software they've designed to
work specifically with their service. This results in
point-and-click access to the full range of Internet
services (see Figure 2.3). Software setup is a snap. You
basically load and install their software, supply your
credit card information, and you are off and running.
We've found that compared to ISPs the only real
drawback to going through a company such as
PSInet/Pipeline is price, which can be somewhat
higher than what an ISP would charge.

For further information, contact:

PSInet/Pipeline: 212.267.3636 or info@pipeline.
com
Netcom: 800.353.6600 or info@netcom.com

When you call for information, ask if you'll be able
to connect to the Internet via a local call from your
location.

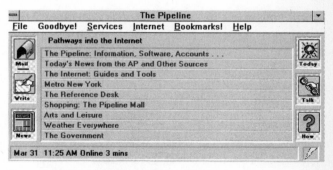

Figure 2.3 PSInet/Pipeline's Opening Screen

INTERNET SEARCH TOOLS

As you learned in Chapter 1, the best part of the
Internet, especially for kids, is the Web. The Web is
growing at a phenomenal rate. At this writing there are

more that 40,000 distinct Web sites, most containing multiple pages. Hundreds of new sites appear each week. To help your child find her way around so she can zero in on sites of interest, we're going to introduce you to two search tools: Yahoo and WebCrawler.

Yahoo
(http://www.yahoo.com/)

Yahoo, from Stanford, is great for browsing the Net.

You can use it to find Web sites by subject category, from Art to Society and Culture, as shown in Figure 2.4. The numbers to the left of each topic indicate the number of Web sites in that category. Once you choose a category of interest, a submenu appears listing specific sites.

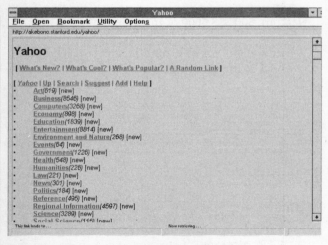

Figure 2.4 Yahoo Subject Category Search Screen

If you have an idea of the site you want to visit, you can also search the Yahoo database by clicking on Search, and entering a term that you believe is found in the URL, title, or comments section of the Web page (see Figure 2.5). We've found that you generally don't have to add the entire URL. Some of them are incredibly long. Just choose some terms from the address;

the more specific, the better. Make sure you've clicked on the URL, Title, and Comments boxes. Now when you click on "Search," Yahoo does the rest.

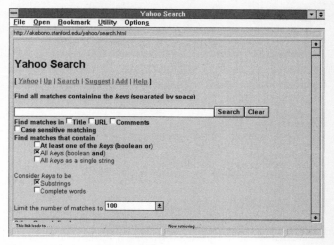

Figure 2.5 Yahoo Search Screen

For every Web site we've described in this book, we've included a URL. These can change. If you find the one we've specified does not call up the site, try a keyword search as we've just described.

For help using Yahoo simply click on "help"; from there you can read the Frequently Asked Questions.

WebCrawler
(http://webcrawler.com/)

Another search tool, and one that's a favorite among some school kids is WebCrawler, Figure 2.6. WebCrawler has a clean, non-intimidating look and feel, which is perfect for kids. They simply enter terms that describe what they are looking for, click on search, and WebCrawler returns with a list of matching "documents." To the left of the list that appears are a series of numbers that indicate how relevant the document is to the query. The numbers range from 0 to 1000, with a score of 1000 indicating the most relevancy.

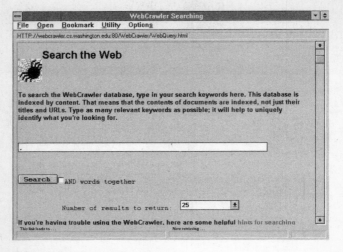

Figure 2.6 WebCrawler Screen

WebCrawler is operated by Brian Pinkerton, a Ph.D. candidate at the University of Washington. Brian feels that kids may want to use Yahoo *and* WebCrawler. Using WebCrawler can be compared to using a library's card catalog. He feels that Yahoo, however, is centered on browsing, so using it is a bit like walking around the stacks.

If your child is not able to find what he or she is looking for using either Yahoo or WebCrawler, there are other tools available, such as Lycos. You can get to these other tools right from Yahoo or WebCrawler—they're linked.

T-MINUS TWO CHAPTERS AND COUNTING

Well, now your spaceship is finished. You have all the tools you'll need for cyberspace travel. Your next stop is Chapter 3, where you'll learn about the different types of online communications and you'll begin to meet some online neighbors. Before you know it, you'll be ready for lift off!

Kidnet

3

Get to Know Your New Neighbors

What kids will do online comes down to one word: communicate. That is, after all, the great draw of the online world, the chance to meet and befriend people from all over the world.

ONLINE COMMUNICATIONS

There are basically four ways to communicate online. Your kids can post messages on public message boards. They can choose specific kids to exchange email with. They can take part in a live interactive chat, or they can attend more formal online conferences.

Message Boards

Message boards can be found in forums and bulletin boards on all of the three major commercial services (see Figure 3.2). They are public areas, and they are

Figure 3.1 Downloaded via Internet from sunsite.unc.edu

often devoted to a particular subject of interest. Each service also has an area, including a message board, devoted just to kids. You'll spend a lot of time in the beginning finding and exploring message boards that interest your kids.

People come online to read their messages and leave postings in response. Using a message board is a great way to get to know other kids and develop keypal relationships with them (the cyberspace version of penpals). By staying in a public forum, your child can get to know others based on their public postings. She can learn about their hobbies and concerns. When the relationship moves to private email in the keypal phase, she will feel like she already knows the other child. This switch from message board to keypal may be quick or it may take some time. Just like in the offline world, friendships sometimes strike like lightning and other times grow like moss. Overall, keypal relationships are more likely to succeed when they grow for a while in a public forum.

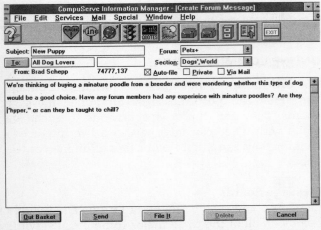

Figure 3.2 A Sample Message Board Posting from CompuServe

Once you've identified the message boards your child likes best, you can let her use them easily, quickly, and inexpensively. Some of the communications software described in Chapter 2 allows you to program your computer to log onto the service, jump from message board to message board automatically downloading new messages, and sign off. Then your child can read the messages offline and prepare responses to be uploaded.

Email

Email is the most popular feature of any online service (see Figure 3.3). It's easy to see why. Email is fast and easy to prepare, and it gets delivered almost immediately. Not only can your child develop keypal relationships with new friends from around the globe, but email can help her keep in touch with her family whether they're in the next state or on the other coast.

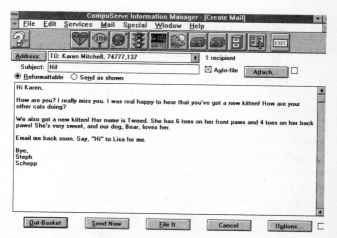

Figure 3.3 A Sample Email Message on CompuServe

Letter writing lost its charm for many of us with the advent of the telephone. Email offers the best of both worlds. It gets delivered quickly, but it retains the charm of the written word. Cyberspace abounds with stories of grandparents who communicate daily with grandchildren across the country, or aunts and uncles who came to know distant nieces and nephews through regular online correspondence. Some distant relatives even believe they learn more about their young family members this way, because the kids feel free to write about things they may not be comfortable revealing face-to-face. Parents traveling on business with their notebook computers in tow also use email to keep in touch with their families back home.

Samantha
CompuServe
Age: 10
London, England

While we were working in the Kids & Teens Student Forum on CompuServe, Samantha invited us to chat. She is so warm and friendly that we instantly decided our readers would like to meet her. Samantha keeps 12 keypals. Ten of these kids live in the United States, one is from Portugal, and one is from Japan. We thought that was a remarkable number of keypals, so we asked Samantha to tell us about how she first came to use online services and how she found so many friends.

My dad showed me this forum, and it looked fun. When I come online, the thing I like to do most is find keypals and talk to people. To find a keypal, I go on the Students Forum and I invite children to talk. If they sound nice, I say, "would you like to be keypals?"

I picked these keypals, because they were nice and friendly. They are all girls. One of them is 18, which is the oldest, and the one who is 9 is the youngest. I don't know how the two kids, who come from countries where they don't speak English, learned to speak English, but I guess they learned in school

I learn about their cultures by asking them questions. I ask what time it is in their country. I ask about their music and other things. They tell me what's different about their country.

Email Pricing

All three major services allow you to send a number of email messages per month as part of their basic rate package. Connect time charges apply for the time you spend in the mail section of the service. Some additional charges can also apply depending on the service and the way your child uses email.

America Online includes unlimited email messages as part of your monthly fee. Your time spent online reading or composing your mail counts as connect time toward your monthly allotment, but you will not be charged per message sent unless your child needs to send a fax or a paper letter generated online. You will be charged $2.00 for each fax and $2.50 for each paper message.

CompuServe also allows you to send unlimited email messages without incurring extra charges. Time spent reading and writing messages online counts against your allotted time. Special types of messages such as Congressgrams are charged at specific rates. GO MAILRATES for complete details.

Prodigy has no monthly limit to the number of messages your child can send. Again, time spent creating and reading mail online counts against your monthly allotment. If you use Prodigy's Mail Manager to prepare email offline, you'll pay 1 cent per 1,000 byte block sent or received. Check for the latest prices when you log on.

Online Chats

Live, interactive online chatting is a thrilling experience. Imagine logging onto your computer and getting invited into a conversation with a child across the ocean. Ethan, age 7, went online with us one day when he was home sick from school. He received an

43

invitation to talk from a girl who lives in Sweden. She was 15, but very willing to chatter away with a little boy across the ocean. She asked him why he wasn't in school, and he asked her if people in Sweden tell stories about vampires. He was very impressed when we used the atlas to show him exactly where Sweden is, and he learned that this girl had never heard a vampire story that was particularly Swedish.

We've uncovered some great places online for your kids to try live chats. They are fun, and it would be a shame to deny your kids this aspect of online communication. Still, live chats come with a couple of cautions. First is a reminder that people can claim to be what they are not when they're online. Live chats should be supervised, at least in the beginning. It is also important that you teach your child how to use the "ignore" feature. The software for every service includes one, and it is a must for live chats. If someone gets obnoxious with your child, show him how to push this button and make the offender disappear!

The other warning is to watch the amount of time and money your child spends in live chats. Yes, it is fascinating to chatter away to new friends from around the world, but the meter is always running. Establish an amount of money you are willing to spend, and then see to it that your child logs off when the allotted time is up.

Live chats can take place in either public chat rooms or in private rooms created by just a few members. The public chat rooms are open to everyone and can contain as many as 25 people. They can get overwhelming. Your child can invite one or several other kids into a private chat room where it's easier to talk.

Instant Messages

America Online and Prodigy allow you to send and receive instant messages to or from anyone else who is currently using the service. Suppose your child is online when the mail icon pops up to indicate a message has been received. When he checks the mailbox, he finds that his friend has just logged on and posted an email message to him. With the press of the Instant Message command, he can contact that friend immediately and begin a live interactive chat. This is a great way for friends to explore the service together.

Kids who use CompuServe can invite each other into live chats when they are in the same forum together, but they cannot invite someone who is elsewhere on the service.

Conferences

Conferences are formal live chats that are usually hosted events and often include a guest speaker. There are countless live conferences online everyday. Check the areas of your child's interest for schedules of upcoming conferences. When the conference begins, all participants gather together in the conference center. The host moderates the proceedings. Your child can submit a question for the guest. His questions will queue with the questions of other guests, and, before too long, he'll see it posted to the guest and get a response. Guests in online conferences come from everywhere. You'll find TV stars, scientists, authors, and sports personalities online for conferences. Budget a few into your child's monthly online budget. It's an experience worth the money.

EMOTICONS AND ACRONYMS

Communicating online is different, not only because it happens so immediately, but because you can't use facial expressions and body language. To spice up their messages, lots of kids like emoticons and acronyms. Here are some to get you started. (Read the emoticons by tilting your head slightly to the left!)

ACRONYMS

BTW	By the way
OTOH	On the other hand
OIC	Oh, I see!
IMHO	In my humble opinion
LOL	Laughing out loud!
ROFL	Rolling on the floor laughing!
G,D&R	Grinning, ducking, and running
[sigh]	Sighing
g	Grinning

EMOTICONS

:-)	I'm happy
:->	Another happy face
:-D	Said with a smile
:-(	I'm sad
(:-(	I'm very sad
(:-.—	I'm crying
(:-&	I'm angry
:-O	I'm shouting
;-)	I'm winking
*:O)	I'm clowning around
=l:-)=	Uncle Sam, I'm patriotic
*<!:-)	I feel like Santa Claus
@>->-	I'm sending you a rose

Member Directories

Every major online service maintains a member directory. It's the telephone book for that part of the online world (see Figure 3.4). When you first sign onto a service, hop over to the member directory and complete an entry for yourself. Basic information often includes your name, online address, hometown and state, and a few of your interests or hobbies. Be careful how personal and specific you make the information for security reasons, but don't hesitate to list yourself in the directory. A complete directory makes it easy for people to find each other and helps build a sense of community online.

Kidnet

46

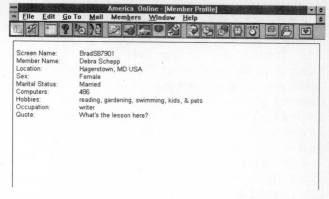

Figure 3.4 Our Member Directory Entry on America Online

You can search the member directory to find other people who share your hometown or interests. It's fun to check for other people with your last name, especially if it's an unusual one.

The member directory is easy to find. On America Online, just pull down the Member menu, and there it is. CompuServe lists it on the Mail pull-down menu. On Prodigy, use the Jump pull-down menu to access the Jump command. Enter the Jump word (MEMBER LIST).

GREAT PLACES TO MEET KIDS ONLINE

We've scouted out some terrific places for your kids to meet other kids online. We chose these spots because they seemed like fun, and they are supervised by grown-ups.

America Online
Kids Only (KIDS)
This is the place to find other kids on America Online. Kids Only is for kids from 5 through 14. It includes active message boards and live chat areas. Although parents are welcome to visit and browse the message boards, they are not permitted to post messages or join in group discussions.

The message boards include Kids Only Funtime and Kids Only Seriously. These headings speak for themselves. Funtime includes lots of talk about kids' favorites and things they think are stupid. (Funny, but these are often the same, depending on who's posting the message!) Seriously includes discussions of divorce, bereavement, and school. Generation to Generation gives kids a place to talk with adults about memories, grandparents, and life in general.

Kids Connection is the live conference area of the Kids Only section. It is devoted to live conversations (see Figure 3.5). Kids gather here to chat, play games, and visit with special guests. Kids Connection is divided into three areas: The Treehouse, the Playground, and the Chat Shack.

The Treehouse is a chat area that is organized and administered by the adult Kids Only staff members. Live chats devoted to special topics are scheduled throughout the week. Chat times are reserved in the Treehouse for members under age 8 or for Star Trek fans, for example. During these chat times, anyone wishing to discuss the scheduled topic is invited to

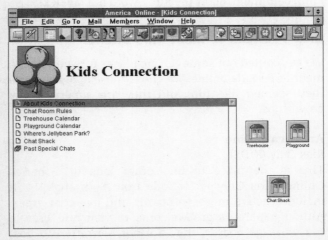

Figure 3.5 The Kids Connection Screen on America Online

attend. The Treehouse is open from 3:00 P.M. till 2:45 A.M. EST on weekdays and from 9:00 A.M. to 2:45 A.M. EST on weekends.

The Playground and the Chat Shack are less structured than the Treehouse. They are reserved for topics chosen by the kids rather than scheduled by the Kids Only staff. The Playground is open daily from 3:00 p.m. to 11:45 p.m. EST. Chat Shack is open daily from 6:00 p.m. to 9:00 p.m. EST.

Teen Scene (TEEN) (T)
Here's the spot for older kids. It features message boards and nightly chats. We include it here, because your 13- and 14-year-olds will probably be curious about it. Message board sections include The Clubhouse for discussing all subjects; likes/dislikes, whatever kids want to talk about. The Pen Pals area is for hooking up with others, and the Movies/Videos/Music section is for swapping reviews and opinions.

Message threads run the gamut from Most Embarrassing Moments, to Parents, to Kissing Tips, to Abortion. Your older kids will find ideas exchanged in strong language, but it probably won't surprise or distress them. If anything, the anonymity of the computer may make it easier for them to explore some of these topics than if they were to try to debate them face-to-face with their friends.

Your younger cybernauts don't belong here. Check it out for yourself before introducing it to your kids. Only you can decide if this area is right for your family.

CompuServe
Kids & Teens Student Forum (STUFOA)
This is CompuServe's online meeting place for students through the high school years. For online friendships, this spot can't be beat. It's filled with friendly, chatty kids. Your kids are likely to receive chat invitations almost as soon as they enter the forum. As a matter of fact, we've never been in this

forum without receiving a friendly invitation to chat. We've talked with teens and younger kids. They are an incredibly friendly group of people.

We met 15- and 16-year-old kids who were more than willing to spend their time online helping our younger kids learn the ropes. We still receive email from some of the kids we met here. This is an excellent place to cut your online conversation teeth. It is well supervised and managed. The message boards are lively. You can feel good about your kids going here to visit without too much worry about who they will bump into or what might happen while they're here.

Prodigy
The Club BB (CLUB) (Plus)
Your kids can meet other kids here on Prodigy. The Club has message boards and live chat areas. The message boards are crammed full of every conceivable topic from Power Rangers to Baby-Sitters Club to Careers and Pen Pal Requests.

Kids can't automatically chat on Prodigy. Only the A member has automatic access to chatting features. Your kids will be B, C, or D members, and you'll have to actually approve their participation in live chats. The problem is, you can't approve chats in only kid-related areas as of this writing. You either allow your child access to all live chats on Prodigy (Don't do it!), or they can't chat at all. The best alternative is to take them to their own live chats, and make sure they don't wander into areas of adult conversation. Leave the chat disabled unless you're planning to be with them.

THE INTERNET

World Wide Web
Find keypals, "visit" other schools, or help your own school make its mark on the Net. The following sites and Net resources explain how.

By the way, there's currently no master directory of Internet users. The best way for your kids to find out if a friend is on the Net is simply to ask him!

Young Person's Guide to Hot Web Spots
(http://www.osc.on.ca/kids.html)

Another page of pages, this one is brief but capti-vating. It features an interesting mix of sites, with an international flair. These include the Korea BBS (con-nect to a keypal in Korea); the Canadian Kids Home page; The Children's Literature Web Guide; a home page from the Rockingham Public School in Halifax. Just to show the Webmaster had a lighter side, there's also a link to the Rolling Stones Web Site.

What's New With NCSA
(http://www.ncsa.uiuc.edu:80/sdg/software/mosaic/docs/whats-new.html)

Parents, this one is a gift to you. *What's New* is the place to check for interesting new sites on the Web, for kids of all ages as they say. It's updated three times a week. Our favorite part is the "Pick of the Week," which is almost always a site we want to explore right away. The week we wrote this, the Seniors Computer Infor-mation Project (SCIP) was highlighted. This site fea-tures links to pages that would interest senior citizens, including "advocacy, health, housing, income, finance, and more."

What's New is a joint project of NCSA, the National Center for Supercomputing Applications, the origina-tors of the popular Mosaic browser software, and O'Reilley & Associates publishers.

Uncle Bob's Kid's Page
(http://gagme.wwa.com/~boba/kids.html)

Described as a "treasure chest of links," this is a great place to get a feel for what's on the Internet for kids (see Figure 3.6). At the time of our review, the "page" had gotten very big and Bob Allison had plans to break it up into more manageable chunks.

Figure 3.6 Uncle Bob's Kid Page

What we liked about this site were the great variety of links it included, everything from science-oriented sites such as Volcano World and Apollo 11, to fun sites such as Froggy, LEGO, and the Unicycling page. He spotlights hot categories such as astronomy, reference works, literature, Disney, and Kids Newsgroups. You won't agree with all of Bob's picks, but he's on the mark often enough to warrant visiting this site regularly.

Kids Web
(http://www.npac.syr.edu/textbook/kidsweb/)
Here you'll find a kids-oriented subset of the Web, with links broken down by subject categories such as The Arts, The Sciences, the Social Sciences, Social Studies, and Miscellaneous.(These broad categories, in turn, are subdivided.) It's easy to navigate, and a little less imposing (but more school-oriented) than Uncle Bob's Kid's page.

The Hotlist of K–12 Internet School Sites
(http://toons.cc.ndsu.nodak.edu/~-sackmann/k12.html)

This is the place to get started when exploring what other schools are doing on the Web. From these sites (there are both non-U.S. and U.S. sites) you can click on a state or country of interest and "visit" schools from near and far.

Hillside Elementary School
(http://hillside.coled.umn.edu)
Hillside Elementary in Cottage Grove, Minnesota, was one of the first elementary schools to establish a Web site. Hillside's site displays the results of its recent Internet research projects. Your kids will enjoy learning about the kids of this progressive school and what they're doing on the Net.

THE KIDS' CHOICE: FAVORITE WEB SITES

Here's a list of favorite web sites from the third graders of Room 12 at the Arbor Heights school in Seattle, Washington. The comments are those of the kids!

Power Rangers Home Page—Oh my goodness! Room 12 will never be the same! Runaway #1 choice!

The Lion King—One of our favorite stops on the WWW! Pictures, movies, even a coloring book!

The White House—Visit the home of our President, hear Socks meow, lots more!

Frog Dissection Page—Lots of graphics about dissecting frogs—not for the squeamish, but a big hit in Room 12!

Interactive Games—We finally caught the "Wumpus," and we sure do enjoy playing Tic-Tac-Toe!

WebCrawler Searching—An easy way to find information on the WWW!

Nickelodeon Shows on the Web—Our favorite is The Rugrats!

On-line Mountain Hop—Beautiful pictures of the Himalayas, the tallest mountains in the world!

Carlos' Interactive Coloring Book—We've had ter-
   rific fun coloring in neat pictures!
Dinosaurs—What a place! Dinosaurs everywhere!
   They run, they talk!

Welcome to the White House
(http://www.whitehouse.gov/)

Stop by the White House, sign the guest book,
leave comments, hear the President's or the Vice
President's welcoming address. The Family Life at the
White House page reads a bit like a Weekly Reader
article, so kids should like it. There are lots of pictures and biographical information. Through this site,
kids can also sift through thousands of government
reports, read recent speeches by the President, and
learn about programs such as the Peace Corps.

KidsCom
(http:/www.spectracom.com/kidscom/)

Billed as a communications playground just for
kids ages 8 to 12, here kids can find keypals with similar interests, post messages on the graffiti wall, play
a geography game, and contribute to a collective
story (see Figure 3.7). Another feature called Ask
Tobie Wan Kenobi allows kids to post questions about
the Internet. Newcomers are asked to register by
filling out a form; providing address information is
optional. Parents are welcome to preview the site
first. The Webmaster would like parents to know that
"the site is heavily monitored, and we do our best to
make sure it is only kids using it."

Global Show-N-Tell
(http://www.manymedia.com/show-n-tell/)

Here's a place for kids to show off their favorite projects and accomplishments to other kids worldwide!
Webmaster David Newman says it's like hanging kids'
artwork on the fridge, only much bigger (see Figure 3.8).

Figure 3.7 KidsCom

When we visited we found a still life from a Canadian girl named Ekaterina; and links to home pages from some creative kids in Oxford, England. There are selections from previous exhibits and full instructions for how to submit your own creation. This site needs to be expanded a bit, but it's still worth a visit.

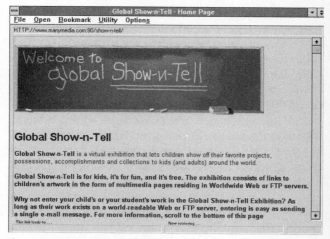

Figure 3.8 Global Show-N-Tell

KidLink
(http://kidlink.cait.duq.eu:70/0/other/gen0001/.html)

KidLink's admirable goal is to start a global dialog that will include as many 10- to 15-year-olds from around the world as possible. The service is free. The only requirement is that kids answer these four questions before participating:

1. Who am I? (Your child describes himself, including his interests, hobbies, etc.)
2. What do I want to be when I grow up?
3. How do I want the world to be better when I grow up?
4. What can I do now to make this happen?

The answers (and they are supposed to be "well-thought-out" and not just a sentence) should then be sent as an email message to: RESPONSE@VM1.NODAK.EDU

Now, your kids are part of KidLink.

The current KidLink project is KIDS—96. Through this, kids can participate in conversations 24 hours a day with other kids worldwide. There are also Kid-cafes, which are mailing lists by which kids exchange messages to other members.

It's easy to get started with this project. We recommend that first you retrieve the file KIDLINK GENERAL, which is the official project introduction. To get your copy, send a message to: LISTSERV@VM1.NODAK.EDU

In the text of the message, write: GET KIDLINK GENERAL. The file will then be sent to you.

KidLink also has its own chat area, where kids can exchange messages in real-time (without any kind of delay). Only registered users can take part in these chats. Kidlink Project Coordinator Odd de Presno tells us that "We've been letting kids chat from the beginning, so I guess that it is safe to claim that we have developed procedures and texts to make it easy for people. Also, we have a team of volunteer helpers eager to help out."

Kidnet

MidLink Magazine
(http://longwood.cs.ucf.edu/~-midlink/)
   This is an electronic magazine for kids 10–15. You'll find examples of art and writing from kids worldwide.

Newsgroups

The following newsgroups are for kids interested in finding keypals and posting messages they feel other kids would be interested in reading.

k12.chat.elementary
csn.ml.k12
   A similar newsgroup, k12.chat.junior, did not appear to be supervised (moderated, in Netspeak) when we checked it out. The postings were perhaps a little too freewheeling for our comfort.

THE BEST OF THE REST

Delphi
The Buddha's Room (CUSTOM FORUMS-BUDDHA)
This is Delphi's forum just for kids between the ages of 10 and 20. It's designed to foster a sense of community among kids, giving them a spot to meet and exchange ideas and feelings freely. It includes a message board, nightly conferences, its own magazine, polls, and Internet access from its menu.

GEnie
The White House (WHITEHOUSE)
Sending a letter to the President or the Vice President couldn't be easier. Just call up a menu, fill out your message, and push a button. It's on its way. As you already know, you can also contact the White House on the Internet.

ONE LAST STOP AND YOU'RE OFF

You've been very patient. By now you have a good idea about what you want to do when you get online.

You know everything you need to know about actually connecting your computer to the online world, and you've met some new neighbors. So why delay? All societies need rules for governing the behavior of their members. The online society is no different. Since you are taking young and uninitiated people into this world, they can be especially naive and vulnerable. Don't go online until you've read through Chapter 4 and learned about some basic rules for safe travel online. Then, from your first visit together, you can be teaching your kids how to behave and how to protect themselves while they're online.

4

Online Rules
of the Road

We know, you're eager to get online. Just as you had to read the driver's manual before you could get your license, you also need to understand some of the basics of traveling online. Then, you'll be able to teach your kids rules for traveling properly in the online world from the start.

THE DRIVER'S MANUAL

Each of the commercial services has features designed to help you get started. No doubt, the first time you logged on you found some screens that provided rules for online behavior. For example, America Online calls this the Terms of Service (TOS). These areas are usually free of connect time charges, and the services encourage you to read the rules listed there and abide by them. We encourage you to print them out and go over them with your kids.

Each service also has files of Frequently Asked

Figure 4.1 Downloaded via Internet from wuarchive.wustl.edu

Questions or FAQs. Remember that millions of new-comers (newbies) have signed on before you. The services have learned what new users need to know, and to keep it simple for everyone, they provide stored files where common beginner's questions are answered based on the experiences of those who came before you. Using the FAQs is especially important on the Internet, where it's considered bad form to pose questions that have been answered many times before.

America Online has its Members' Online Support (HELP), as shown in Figure 4.2. This is a free service where you will find information about access speeds, passwords, and parental control options. You can also stop here for live technical support, or to leave messages asking other members for help with specific problems.

Figure 4.2 America Online's Member Services Screen

CompuServe's New Member Welcome Center (WELCOME), shown in Figure 4.3, is a good place for the newcomer to look for help. Here you will find service highlights, the new member forum, and the new member help desk. You can get to CompuServe's Frequently Asked Questions by entering (ANSWERS), and if you take the new member survey, giving CompuServe some information about your needs and habits, they will reward you with $5.00 of connect time. Plus, you guessed it, time spent in these areas is free.

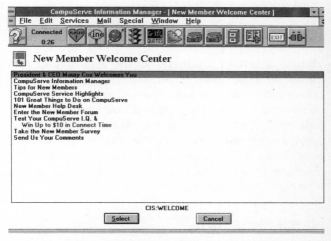

Figure 4.3 New Member Welcome Center on CompuServe

Prodigy's online help features are accessible from the Member Help Center hot button on the main menu. This area provides tutorials for learning how to navigate the service, billing information, and custom options to personalize your screens and toolbars. Time spent in the Member Help Center is free.

All of the commercial services offer free online tours to help you learn your way around. America Online's tour begins when you enter the keyword (TOUR). This trip takes you through highlights of 12 features on America Online. CompuServe's tour is also accessed by entering the Go word (TOUR). From Prodigy's Member Help Center, click on the hot button Getting Around. You will begin a tour to explain how Prodigy's menus work and how the service is organized.

So, when you explore these services, use the help that is already in place. Don't sit and wonder where the answers are. You'll find that the things that confound you have confounded millions of others before you. Commercial services want to be friendly and accessible. They are the experts in using their services, after all, and besides, it's free!

TRAVEL TOGETHER

The vehicle you constructed in the last chapter was meant to hold two. We encourage you to explore cyberspace with your kids. There is so much for all of you to learn and enjoy. This is a new opportunity for kids and parents to learn, discover, and grow together. Besides, while you're exploring together, your child may never notice that you are also teaching him to travel safely and contribute to his new community wisely.

WATCH THOSE TOLLS

From your very first online session together, you should be teaching your kids that in the online world, time is money. You, no doubt, have a few hours of free exploring time as a new member of whichever services you've joined. That's great. But, free time dissolves very quickly in this fascinating new world. If you and your child aren't careful, your first month online may also be your last.

How are you going to feel next month when your credit card bill arrives, including $162.59 for time spent online? For some families, that is the end of their cyberspace adventure.

This won't happen to you if you are aware of the potential danger and prepare to prevent it. To help you do this, we recommend you create a usage log to use with your free time. Each time you log on, you can use the log to note the time you started your session, the areas you visited, your feelings about those areas, and the time you logged off. Using the usage log conscientiously will let you know exactly when your free time is gone. A carefully maintained usage log will also become your own personal map. Looking over the log will help you see just where you've been, how much you enjoyed your visit, and what, if anything you might want to do in that area next.

The commercial services help you keep track of your online time. America Online's software includes a little clock on the tool bar. Click on this to see what the current time is and how long you've been online during the current session. CompuServe's CIM software features a running clock in the left corner of your screen so that you know exactly how long you've been logged on. To check you online time on Prodigy, click on the T for Tools on the bar at the bottom of your screen. Then you can choose Session Timer to see how long you've been logged on.

Work Offline; Visit Online

From your first trip online, you and your kids can develop some good habits that will help you to control costs. If you use CompuServe or America Online, never, ever compose email messages online or read your mail with the meter running. The software for both services allows you to compose email messages offline and then go online only to send them. The programs also allow you to jump onto the services, scoop up the contents of your mailbox and log off to read the messages. Now you can linger over the words and thoughts of your online friends. You can write and edit your prose, endlessly and for free. When you're ready to send your mail, simply dial out again. Using this technique conscientiously will allow you to send email with connect time charges that run in minutes rather than hours.

If your software doesn't offer this function, look for a "navigator" program online. The software libraries of the major commercial services are full of programs that will automate your email. On CompuServe, look for TAPCIS or NAVCIS. Prodigy users can download Prodigy's Mail Manager, a DOS-based program available through Prodigy. You can always go to the New Member Help area and ask for directions. Before you know it, you will have downloaded the software, installed it, and gotten your email costs under control.

Save Your Favorites
You'll develop favorite online destinations; places you visit almost every trip online. Most communications software allows you to store those places and their locations for quick access, for example, CompuServe's Favorite Places menu (see Figure 4.4). Other software programs may call these bookmarks. They make it very easy for you to hop online and scoot around to your favorite spots. They also provide a nice profile of how your family uses its online time.

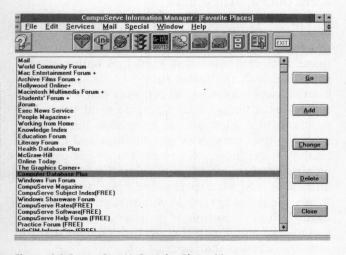

Figure 4.4 CompuServe's Favorite Places Menu

TRAVEL SAFELY

Magazines and newspapers are full of stories about kids and the dangers they face online. Can these dangers be real? Absolutely. Are they overplayed in the press? Absolutely. The online world is a vast and diverse one. The large commercial services have millions of subscribers. At any time, you and your kids are likely to be online in the company of hundreds of thousands of other people. Some of them may be folks you don't want to know. The online world is as exciting and enriching as Manhattan, and it can also be as unseemly.

Do you think your children should avoid Manhattan at all costs? Manhattan has some tough and nasty areas, certainly unsuitable for kids to explore alone. Would you be satisfied if they never saw the Metropolitan Museum of Art in order to make sure they were always spared from Time Square? We didn't think so. Instead, you'd take them to Manhattan yourself. You'd show them what you wanted them to see, and you'd avoid the areas that make you nervous. You'd also teach them some coping techniques; give them some guidelines for looking out for themselves. You're going to do this online, too!

Know Where You Are
For years you've been making choices for your kids about what you want in their lives and what you don't. When you first go online, know what you're looking for. That's why we wrote this book! It's filled with recommended stops for you to enjoy with your kids. Plan what you want to do before you log on. Jot down stops to explore for each session. Once you learn your way around a little, you'll have fun exploring new areas and discovering favorites of your own, and some of these discoveries will be delightfully unexpected. But, by then you and your kids will feel at home. You'll be experienced enough to be able to spot trouble, should it arise.

Know Who is There With You

All the major commercial services have online support people in place who know their areas and know the people who frequent them. As long as your kids stick to places that are intended for younger "cybernauts," there will be adults present to look out for them.

When you and your child go into a new forum or bulletin board, seek out the administrator or "sysop" as part of your initial visit. You may actually find this person online when you're there, but even if you don't, you'll find an address for getting in touch through email. Forums and message boards always list their staff members so you'll easily see who is in charge.

Introduce yourself and your kids. Give this person some information about what you want your kids to take from their online experiences and what you may be worried about. These folks are here because they care about kids and they care about the online world. They are very willing to keep an eye on what is happening online, and they are very happy to help a newcomer find her way. When Richard, of London, England, first decided to take his girls online, they stopped in the Kids and Teens Student Forum on CompuServe. Samantha, age 10, left some messages on the message board. The next day, a sysop returned one message, because she had included her address in it. Richard thought, "That's sensible," so his girls are free to explore in this forum to their hearts' content, under the watchful eyes of the forum's staff.

TEN RULES FOR STAYING SAFE ONLINE

1. Know if your communication is in a public message area or a private one. Message boards are public, so are conferences, and many live chats. Whatever you say in these settings is the same as shouting it in the middle of a crowded mall. Email is private and so are invitation-only chats and instant messages.

Instant messages are messages sent to someone who you know is also online when you are. They are the online equivalent of whispering in your friend's ear.

2. Never post personal information in public messages. Personal information includes your address, phone number, your employer, and the name of your child's school.

3. Teach your kids to never reveal your family's schedule and routines. No one needs to know when you get home from work vs. when they get home from school. No one needs to know when you're going on vacation.

4. Remind kids that online communication is faceless, and people may not actually be who they say they are. Teach them to be alert for anything that doesn't "feel" right, and make sure they report these events to you immediately.

5. Teach your kids that they must never respond to someone who is trying to bother them online. Software programs from the major commercial services include "Ignore" commands for live chats. If someone says something that bothers you or your child, put them on ignore, and they'll just disappear. You can also teach your kids to make people disappear by just logging off, or in a real pinch, shut off the computer. If you receive unsettling email, forward it to the service personnel, and they'll track down the person who sent it.

6. Make sure your kids never plan to meet their online friends face-to-face without your permission and input. Your child may make a friend he wants to meet in person, but that meeting should be under your supervision.

7. If you arrange a real-life meeting, make sure your first meeting is in a public place, and make sure all parents are present. Arrange to meet at the park or at a pizza parlor. This way, all parties can get to know each other before revealing the locations of their homes.

8. Never let your child reveal your password. No one ever needs this information. Sometimes people will pose as employees of the online service you're using. They may try to tell you about some problem with your account that requires your password for them to investigate. They are full of bologna. No service employee will ever ask for your password.

9. Change your password periodically so that potential criminals won't have time to figure it out. Some people have actually developed their own software programs for randomly figuring out other peoples' passwords. Then they use these passwords to run up huge bills. Although such crimes are not common, why not protect yourself if you can?

10. Check your billing information frequently so that you'll know what your charges are, and you'll be alert to any possible misuse.

PARENT AS TRAFFIC COP

Some of the commercial services have parental control options that you can exercise to prevent your kids from having complete access to every part of the service. These options usually control live chatting and participation on bulletin boards. They are very useful for protecting your child and keeping her out of areas where kids don't really belong, but you can overdo parental controls, disabling features your kids might really enjoy. For example, if you don't allow your child to attend conferences, an option on America Online, she may miss the chance to attend a meeting that could be both enjoyable and educational. Of course, you wouldn't want her to find her way into a singles' live chat. You'll have to strike the balance for yourself.

America Online's parental controls, the hot button for which is shown in Figure 4.5, are specific to the service's real-time live features. You can completely disable your child's access to the People Connection live chat feature, or you could disable just the member-created rooms where private chats occur in the People Connection. You can block your child's access to all conferences and role-playing games. You can also block instant messages, so that your child can't receive invitations to private chats. These last two options are extreme. Blocking conferences means your child can't attend any online meetings, some of which can be quite useful. Blocking instant messages means that your kids can't respond to a live chat invitation if one of their keypals happens to find them online.

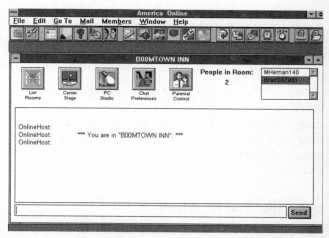

Figure 4.5 Live Chat Room Showing the Parental Control Hot Button on America Online

Prodigy offers the head of the family, the A member, the opportunity to block out access to service areas for the subordinate members. Figure 4.6 shows Prodigy's Household Member Access Screen. You can jump (CHANGE ACCESS) to see a list of bulletin boards. Then you can go through the list and enable or block the access of your children's passwords according to where you want and don't want them to visit.

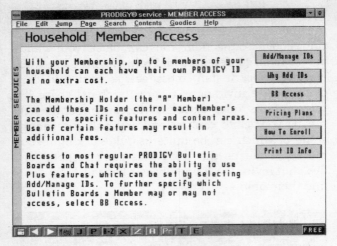

Figure 4.6 The Household Member Access Screen on Prodigy

Parental control features are easy to use, and you'll find them with other member support features. Commercial services are very aware of parents' concerns about the safety of the online world, so check for new parental controls when you go online.

OBEY THE TRAFFIC RULES

Just as you have concerns for your kids online, the other folks online want to travel through a safe and friendly community, too. Rules for online behavior are commonly called netiquette. Teach them to your children from the beginning, and they will be welcome in any online community. These rules are important enough for you to enforce strongly. We recommend that you work with your child to draft a contract of rules and expectations about online usage and behavior. You are the only one who can do this, because these rules must reflect the values that you are putting in place for your kids. Once you have decided, based on our recommendations and some

Kidnet

ideas of your own, what you expect of your kids online, make sure they comply. We recommend that you actually create a document that you and your kids all sign. Then post it near the computer as a road sign to help them remember. In the long run, they would much rather have you enforce these rules strongly than to be censured and excluded from the exciting online community by the service staff who disapprove of their behavior.

NETIQUETTE FOR KIDS

Rilla Moulden, of CompuServe's YDrive has been online with kids for years. She keeps a file in the Forum's library of online tips for kids. We thought they were sensible, and she was kind enough to allow us to share them with you. We added a few of our own.

1. DON'T TYPE IN ALL CAPS!!! It looks like you're shouting, and it annoys people.
2. In live chats, don't hold your finger down on the [Enter] key. It ties things up and keeps people from being able to have their say.
3. Don't use nasty language, not even with symbols in place of some of the letters.
4. Think ahead of time about potential unpleasant situations and how to deal with them. The anonymity of the computer allows some people to be crude, rude, and downright nasty at times. Never feel obligated to answer unsolicited mail, messages, or "Talk Box" invitations.
5. Be yourself. It is sometimes very tempting to hide behind your computer monitor and become someone who you really aren't. People sometimes use the cover of their computers to change age, sex, profession, and even their "personality." Remember that on the other side of that screen is a person, just like you. Give someone the chance to know you for who you really are.

6. Show respect for others and the online environment. Just as you would not walk into a public building or the mall shouting profanities, don't pollute the online environment with verbal garbage or childish behavior.

7. Know your limits. Your online time will be a lot more fun if you set your limits ahead of time and stick to them. It is easy to become addicted to online chats and messaging and before you know it, your bill (or your parent's bill) can skyrocket to unreasonable levels. Plan ahead of time which conferences you would like to participate in, and then use a timer to help you stick to the time limit that you've set for yourself.

8. Where there's a flame, there's a fire. Some people visit online communities for the sole purpose of taking out all their frustrations on someone they don't have to face eye-to-eye. If you have a legitimate complaint or a passionate cause, by all means express it! But remember, attack ideas, not people. Disagreement is a way to grow and learn.

9. Everyone was new sometime. Remember the first day you logged on? How confusing it all was! Remember the first person who left you a message or invited you into a talk? Don't forget what it felt like to be new, and help welcome others into the community the way you were once welcomed.

10. Everyone's an expert; but not everyone always knows what they are talking about. Online advice is one of the most compelling benefits of participating in an online community, but always remember that you must ultimately be the one to figure out what is right for you. You will hear lots of advice and lots of different opinions. It is your responsibility to sort it all out.

11. Online people are real and have real feelings. When you interact with people on the computer, even though you can't see them and may never meet them in person, they are real people, with real ideas and real feelings. Treat them with respect and love, just as you would your face-to-face friends.

12. Get to know the staff. Staff members are volunteers who enjoy spending time online communicating with and helping others. They don't have all the answers, but they sure will try to find them for you if they can.

13. Share and share alike. The beauty of an online community is the quality and quantity of information that is exchanged there! That information, in the form of messages and library files, comes from you, the members. Uploading, or sending files from your computer to the service's online libraries is free of connect time charges. If you write poems or reviews of your favorite movies, for example, you can contribute them for free. The forum staff members, like Rilla who gave us these guidelines, are always available through email to help you figure out how to upload a file.

_____

HOW TO SPOT TROUBLE SIGNS

As with many other things available to us, opportunities for abusing online time do exist. Unfortunately we have all heard the stories about kids who get lost in the technology and fail to thrive in the real world. Once your kids get comfortable online, they will surely venture into their favorite areas without you. That's fine for both you and them, but it does bring new concerns to light. As parents, we can do some things to prevent technological tragedies.

We recommend that the computer you use for online exploration be placed in a public part of the house such as the living room or family room. That way, you'll notice if your kids start spending too much time online, before you get the bill. If you tuck it away in your child's bedroom, you may lose track of exactly how long he stays logged on.

In a public location, you can also check in more readily when the kids are online. You can glance at the screen as you go past and take a peek at what they are doing. They'll know you're there if they should come across something that upsets or disturbs them. You can be available to them to help them deal with the situation, or simply tell them to log off.

Notice if your child is beginning to spend less time with her "offline" friends. Online communication should never take the place of friendships that we form face-to-face; it should only complement them. If your child seems to be drifting more toward her online friends, encourage her to spend less time logged on. Schedule some real-life events or outings with her old friends to help her reconnect with them.

Don't let your kids neglect the physical activity they need. Between school, homework, the computer, video games, and TV, your kids can neglect their cardiovascular systems. Limit their online time just as you would their TV time. An hour a day is probably sufficient.

Check your hard drive every once in a while for graphic image files. They often have file extensions of .GIF or .JPEG after the filenames, for example, kids.gif. (A brand new file format, called PNG, may have replaced GIF by the time you read this.) These are usually large—50,000 bytes and more. Aside from the fact that you'll need to keep an eye on them to preserve your disk space, it's possible for your innocent 12-year-old boy to download R-rated or even X-rated images. This is especially important when you're accessing the Internet, where thousands of risqué images are available, if you only know where to find them.

Try to keep some perspective. Just because something happens through this fascinating new technology, doesn't mean it's intrinsically dangerous. Yes, your clever 12-year-old son may find a way to download some pictures you don't want him to see, but to be honest, maybe his dad got hold of some picture at that age that Grandpa didn't want him to see either.

In the end, nothing is foolproof. You have to teach your kids what you expect of them online. Show them, by your example, how responsible people behave online, and make sure they understand the consequences of not abiding by the standards you set. Then, just as in the real world, the moment comes when you have to trust them and the job you've done in teaching them, and let them go. With the tools you'll give them and the time you spend teaching them, they'll be just fine.

RULES FOR THE INTERNET

Everything we've said above applies to the Internet, only more so. As we've said, the Internet is untamed and unmanaged. There's no one looking out for kids, so you'll have to do it. Younger children should not even use the Internet without you. There are too many places for them to go astray and read and see things they shouldn't. Pre-teens should be given strict guidelines as to what's off limits and what's not.

Internet Netiquette

It's too bad, but many Internet users seem to feel that the Internet was better off when it was a relatively closed society, and pretty much the province of academia and government. Therefore, they have little tolerance for the waves of newbies who flooded the Net when the commercial online services such as America Online gave their members easy access.

In part, we can understand where this animosity came from. A lot of these new users jumped right into the Net before bothering to learn the lay of the land. They posted inappropriate messages, sometimes in inappropriate places, and basically acted like tourists. It took Net veterans longer to navigate the Internet because system resources were strained under the load. It was difficult for old-timers to see any advantage in having these new users on the Internet.

There are some simple things you and your child can do to both get the most out your time on the Net, and spare yourselves the grumblings of experienced users, who may feel they have better things to do than show newcomers around. If you will be accessing the Internet through a commercial service such as America Online, be sure to read the helpful files made available about the Internet and its resources. Even Internet service providers, such as PSI's Pipeline, offer files and helpful information—it's all available online, and you only need to look for it.

The FAQs of Internet Life

Also be sure you've read the Frequently Asked Questions files that pertain to the newsgroup you're checking out. Some of the Internet's Web sites also offer FAQs. It's likely they will contain answers to the questions you've thought of, or that would eventually have come to you. FAQs or similar information may be just a click away once you are on a Web site. Also, these sites frequently make it simple to pose a question to the Webmaster (the person who maintains and updates the site) by clicking on his or her name to pull up a form for posing questions. Just who the Webmaster is will vary with the Web site. If it's from a company, for example, the Webmaster is likely to be an employee. Each distinct Web site has it's own Webmaster, although some Webmasters run more than one site. Be certain you've explored any available FAQs before asking the human.

FAQs can be a tremendous information resource. FAQs from the rec.pets.dogs newsgroup, for example, cover medical information, lists of publications, dog-related mailing lists, and information about caring for new puppies. Encourage your child to read the FAQs for the newsgroups she monitors. They are usually posted periodically to the newsgroup itself. Newsgroup FAQs are also available through a Web site:

(http://www.cis.ohio-state.edu:/hypertext/faq/usenet/FAQ-List.html)

You can retrieve the FAQs from this site by searching via keyword or by going through the alphabetized listing of newsgroups.

TEN COOL THINGS YOU CAN DO ONLINE RIGHT NOW

1. Send email to the President. His Internet address is president@whitehouse.gov. Chapter 3 will tell you anything else you might need to know.
2. Have a live conversation with a distant new friend. Chapter 3 will tell you all about online chatting, and you'll find a few good places to start visiting online.
3. Find a joke. Chapter 13 will tickle your funny bone. You'll find places to look for jokes, comic strips, and funny stories.
4. Read one of your favorite magazines. Online magazines for kids, such as Disney Adventure or Sports Illustrated, are all over cyberspace. Check out Chapters 5, 6, and 8 just to get started.
5. Get a game. See Chapter 14 for some ideas about games we like and how you can find them.
6. Visit a remote school. In Chapter 5 you'll learn about how going online can help with homework and schoolwork. You'll also meet some students who have put their classrooms into cyberspace. Drop in for a visit.
7. Explore a family vacation spot. In Chapter 6, you'll see how to check out the latest from the Disney resort world. Chapter 12 will show you how to get the facts about hundreds of cities around the world. You'll find information about popular museums and family attractions in Chapter 10, and you'll also see how you can explore the rain forest, the Arctic, Antarctica, and volcanoes.
8. Get that book report or school project finished! You'll find dozens of ideas for getting that schoolwork done in Chapter 5.

9. Go to the movies. Once the homework is done, check out Chapter 6. You can find still photos, videos, and sound files from most of your favorite current movies. You'll see how to get biographical information about your favorite stars, and you'll learn how to jump into a discussion about your favorite movie or star.

10. Write to us! We'd love to hear what you think as you travel through cyberspace. See page xviii for our online addresses.

5

School
(Have You Done Your Homework Yet?)

By now you've read all about cyberspace, and you've seen some of the wonderful stuff here for kids. Before you go online to play, let's take a look at that homework and see what we can find online to help your kids in school.

Any online service you choose offers an online encyclopedia. Your kids can work with other groups of kids on science projects. They can visit some of the world's most famous museums, and they can search some of the world's greatest libraries. They can even get a teacher to help them with an assignment they don't understand.

Using online services to help your kids in school is a subject worthy of its own book. Since we only have a chapter to devote to it, we'll highlight some of the best we've found and let you go exploring for the rest. We've tried to stick close to the things designed just for kids, but the offerings are so

Figure 5.1 Downloaded via Internet from wuarchive.wustl.edu

intertwined, that we also included some sites for teachers.

If you're one of the growing number of parents who homeschools your kids, you will discover a whole new world of educational opportunities online.

AMERICA ONLINE

Academic Assistance Center (AAC, HOMEWORK)

The Academic Assistance Center is the place to go for help with all types of school- and homework-related problems and questions (see Figure 5.2). You will find 780 staff members ready to help your kids with everything from that algebra homework to the end-of-term research project. You and your kids can feel confident about the help you receive here. More than 40 percent of the staff members hold doctorate degrees, and 75 percent of them have at least a masters. Just a warning, these are experienced teachers; they won't solve your problem for you anymore than your child's own teacher will. They'll give you the help and guidance you need to do it yourself, but they won't do your homework for you! Help is available in three ways.

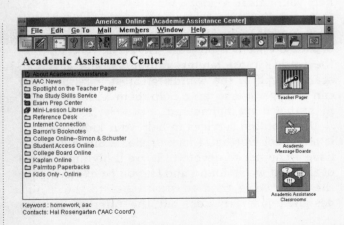

Figure 5.2 The Academic Assistance Center on America Online

Real Help in Real Time

The first place you should stop for homework help is in one of the three live chat rooms. Here you will find teachers waiting to offer you live, immediate, online help. The Academic Assistance Room is for general help, and you will find a teacher here throughout the whole day. If you have a homework problem, just drop in and ask about it. The teacher will either be able to help you, or recommend an online or offline reference that will help. Weekly schedules list tutoring sessions for specific subjects throughout the week. If your child is having trouble in a particular class, check it out and drop in for special tutoring. The other two chat rooms are the Humanities Room and the Math and Science Room. They provide subject-specific help.

Page A Teacher

If the teacher in the chat room can't help, you can page a teacher who can. The Teacher Pager is a hot button on the main screen of the Academic Assistance Center, but the feature is also available from any part of America Online. Simply enter the keyword teacher pager and the Pager mail form will appear (see Figure 5.3). Complete the mail form, listing your child's question, her grade level, and the subject of the question. Once you send the form, it will go to a central coordinator who will review it and direct it to a teacher experienced in the subject you're asking about.

The teacher who receives your page will review it and get back to you with help. That help may be an email message that includes specific advice, or it could be an offer to meet with you online in the Homework Help room for a live chat. When you send a Teacher Pager message, you should stay online for a minute or two. That gives the coordinator a chance to get back to you immediately if necessary. If you've waited a couple of minutes without a response, don't hang online for no reason. Just check back later for an email message. Your question is guaranteed to be answered within 48 hours, and in most cases it will be more like 6 to 12 hours.

We decided to give the Teacher Pager a try, so we posed a fourth grade science question. We were looking for a list of deciduous and fir trees native to our home state of Maryland. We went online right after school, about 4:00 P.M. EST. Within an hour we received a notice telling us that our question had been forwarded to a teacher. Before bedtime, we had a reply listing some field guides specific to our part of the country that would give us the information we needed. These books are readily available at any good library. We knew exactly what we had to do next to finish the assignment.

The popularity of the Teacher Pager feature has exploded in the last few years. In 1993, the teachers were processing 10 to 15 pages a day. By 1995, that had grown to more than 300 a day! The system has grown to keep up with the demand, and by the end of 1995, the teachers expect to be able to answer over 2,000 questions a day.

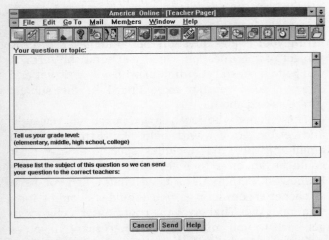

Figure 5.3 The Make a Page Screen of the Teacher Pager on America Online

The busiest time for the Teacher Pager is, not surprisingly, between 5:00 P.M. EST and 11:00 P.M. EST, when the service receives 70 percent of its daily requests. Submitting your question during off hours may speed your response even further.

As of this writing, plans were in the works to create a searchable database from the best questions users have asked the teachers over the years. This database will be keyword searchable, allowing you to see answers the teachers have already given based on just a few search words. Look for this when you stop by the Academic Assistance Center, because it is probably finished by now.

Homework Help on the Board
For less immediate help, you can leave messages on the Academic Message Boards. You'll find these on the Academic Assistance Center main menu. There are folders here for every kind of academic question you can pose, from math to history to exam tips and techniques. Students of all ages and teachers share ideas and information freely. These discussions include contests, chats, and questions. Contest winners can earn free online time if they're fast and smart. If you post a specific question about homework, it will most likely be forwarded to a volunteer teacher and you will receive a private email in response. If you post a message in any of these areas and don't get a response within 48 hours, you'll earn 1 hour of free time online.

Scholastic Network (SCHOLASTIC)
Scholastic is a famous name in education, and the Scholastic Network is its online home (see Figure 5.4). Designed for K–12 educators and students, your child will find it a fascinating place to visit. There are standard features and special events planned throughout the entire year. When you first go to the Scholastic Network, you will find a preview screen. Scholastic Network is available through America Online, but it

carries its own monthly subscription fee. For an additional $7.00 per month, you receive 5 hours of time to spend on the Network. Subscribing to the Scholastic Network is like choosing to get a premium cable channel, only much more educational.

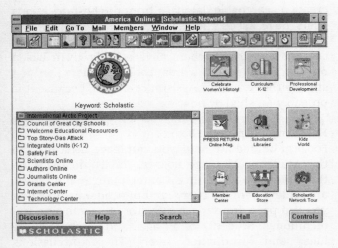

Figure 5.4 The Scholastic Network Online Screen on America Online

Take the preview tour to decide for yourself, but we think it's money well spent. Scholastic Network offers some of what's best about taking your kids online, and you can recover the cost by skipping two trips to the fast-food restaurant a month.

Authors Online

Scholastic is known for its authors, and many of the most famous will meet your kids here on the Network. Todd Strasser, author of *Home Alone* and *Free Willy*, held a writing workshop online. Newberry Medal winner Katherine Paterson, author of *Bridge to Terabithia* and *Jacob, Have I Loved*, has been a guest and so has Frank Asch (a personal favorite), the author of the Bear and Little Bird books. Whether

Kidnet

your child is in preschool or high school, he can read a book in the morning and be chatting in a live conference with the author in the afternoon!

Some Special Events
Every month throughout the school year the Network hosts a special event. The first time we visited, the monthly special focused on America's living Presidents. Each President's biography was available along with highlights of his administration and important news events of his time. More importantly, President Bush and President Carter held live conferences on the Network, and answered questions submitted by students to the message boards. The response was so overwhelming that the questions and answers were still available in the middle of March, although by then the special program was about Women's History Month.

In addition to the monthly special event, Scholastic frequently hosts other events too. Who wouldn't like to take a trip with a dog sled team across the North Pole? How many of us ever will? The International Arctic Project (IAP) began in March 1995, and Scholastic Network made it possible for kids to tag along.

The IAP is an international team of 2 women and 4 men who made the first surface crossing of the Arctic Ocean by dogsled in a single season. The trip covered 2,000 miles of solid and broken sea ice from Russia to Canada across the North Pole, and ran from March through July. Thirty-three dogs pulled the 1,100 pound sleds during the journey.

Before the expedition began, team members met in live conferences online to discuss the trip with the kids. Special meetings with the dog trainers gave them detailed insights into how the dogs were trained and how they would be cared for during the trip.

When the expedition began, the team took communications tools and computers packed on their sleds. This made it possible for the explorers to send daily reports from their expedition to the Scholastic Network. Every week, selected questions submitted by students were forwarded to the expedition, and their answers were posted online. We're willing to bet that this is the closest our kids will come to an Arctic expedition for quite some time, but it should keep them happy!

Lindsey
CompuServe, 74543,1406, America Online, the Internet
Age: 13
Home: Maineville, Ohio, USA
Lindsey is a homeschooler and a self-proclaimed "cyberhead." We first met her in the Dinosaur Forum on CompuServe where she is a regular contributor. She has conceived and helped to design contests and games that have now become regular features in the forum. She loves dinosaurs, and plans to be a "published, successful writer" when she grows up. We chose to profile Lindsey because she is going online to achieve her educational goals in ways we thought you'd like to share with your kids. Here's her story.

On CompuServe, besides the DinoForum libraries and message boards, I use private email extensively to converse with online friends. Also, I enjoy browsing through the message boards and libraries in forums such as New Age, Literary, Writer's, Mensa, Science/Fiction/Fantasy, Astronomy, Living History, and Role-Playing Adventures. I frequently use the download features of CIM as well as the filing cabinet and address book. Upon occasion, I have arranged to meet friends online in chats and often attend conferences, especially in the DinoForum.

On America Online, I enjoy the newsgroups, Scholastic Network, and especially Hatrack, a community of made-up characters who live and work in a fabled village. Orson Scott Card is a writer I really enjoy. This community is his creation, and he participates actively.

I'm also learning about FTP, telneting, gopher, WWW, and other Internet services.

I estimate that I spend approximately one-half hour per day actually connected via modem; however, when conferencing or "playing in traffic" (surfing the Net) my connect time may extend to an hour or more. Further, I spend approximately one-half hour per day maintaining the DinoKids columns and responding to my email, but this is offline time. I'm busy. G

I love to write and have hooked up with several writers. We critique each other's work and offer suggestions/advice/solace. I'm writing a story with a couple of email pals; we are each doing "bits" and combining them into a coherent whole. Challenging and fun! Online writers have graciously critiqued my work and are helping me hone my skills and gain confidence. My mom insists on all the writing conventions like correct grammar, punctuation, spelling, paragraphing, etc., in EVERYTHING I post online. Woof.

On America Online, I can talk about books I'm reading with other homeschoolers and even join them weekly for a chat. I can download lots of information from ERIC and the Scholastic Network. Right now, they are conversing with Presidents Carter and Bush. I'm waiting for Shakespeare.

I can access weekly newsmagazines and daily newspapers, saving my mom a trip to the library. I also get other research material from Net sites. This summer, I will be taking a "Writing the Novel" course online, and next year I will be taking further coursework from universities offering distance learning.

As for researching dinosaurs, I can ask a question about Oviraptor and have a researcher on-site answer it! The challenge of choosing, researching, and writing about a couple of different dinosaurs each week has exposed me to the vast vaults of information available—both accurate and inaccurate, current and out of date. I am fascinated by the idea of identifying a dinosaur by only its braincase and understanding its speed of travel from footprints. Did you know they have actually determined the size, configuration, and diet from only a footprint?

Having to find a unique way to present Guest Dinosaur each week for the DinoForum (i.e., through a poem, a short story, or a word puzzle) has forced me to stretch my writing skills, abandon the usual, and discover forgotten and lesser-known dinosaurs like Opisthicaudia, Pachycephalosaurus, Ouranosaurus, Mamenchisaurus, and Troodon. In this discovery, I've really come to respect those cool Mesozoic dudes. G

Finally, being online has given me lots of opportunities to deal with all kinds of people, and this has aided in my social skills and understanding and enjoyment of the differences in people. Although these skills would be helpful in any career, since I want to be a successful and PUBLISHED author—these opportunities are wonderful!

And so are you, Lindsey.

Smithsonian Online (SMITHSONIAN)

The Smithsonian Institution has an online home on America Online. If you are planning a trip to Washington, you'll want to stop here first and plan your visit to the museums. If a trip to Washington is not in your future, you can peruse some of the exhibits and collections for yourself right here online.

If your child is interested in art, you can tour the galleries of the American Art Museum and download images of some famous works of American art. A sample of the online galleries includes the African-American gallery, the Hispanic Art gallery, American Landscapes, and Women Artist's gallery. There are detailed directions for downloading and viewing these .GIFs, and if the printed directions aren't sufficient for you, you can request help from the staff. The menus also include hot buttons that will direct you to the Graphics forums where you will get expert guidance in the technical aspects of using these files.

You can also tour the National Museum of American History (NMAH) to view images of the First Ladies' dresses, President Lincoln's silver service, a figure from Uncle Tom's Cabin, and other artifacts of American history and culture. The NMAH has a fascinating message board that is very active. Here, students can ask questions of historians, teachers, and history buffs. Research requests abound, and the answers are fast and detailed. If your child is into history, take her here!

Information files will give you information about the Air & Space Museum, the American Indian Museum, The Cooper-Hewitt, Museum of Design, the Natural History Museum, and even the National Zoo.

Library of Congress (LIBRARY)

Online services make the Library of Congress almost as accessible as your local library (see Figure 5.5). Through the Internet, you can access the Library's card catalogue, and we will discuss this feature further later on in this chapter. We are including a discussion of the Library of Congress, as it is available through America Online, because it is well organized and enjoyable, and because not everyone is going to venture onto the Internet.

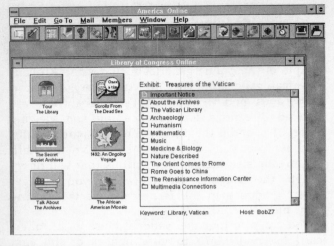

Figure 5.5 The Library of Congress Online on America Online

The Library of Congress on America Online offers you a glimpse of some of the Library's most famous collections. These are presented in a well organized and browsable way. Let's look at an example; The African-American Mosaic. The Mosaic is a library-wide resource guide to the Library's vast collection of books, periodicals, prints, photographs, music, film, and recorded sound.

In 1996, the Library of Congress will mount a major exhibition and cultural program to examine the impact of African-American history and tradition in the formation of the American national identity. The Mosaic online coincides with the preparation of this exhibit. Hot buttons allow your child to read about American historical issues such as the African colonization movement, abolition, and the migration of Black Americans from the farms of the South to the cities of the North. The People's Gallery is a message exchange area for discussing the exhibit as you explore.

You will find similar offerings for other Library collections including The Dead Sea Scrolls, The Secret

Soviet Archives, and 1492: An Ongoing Voyage. The Tour of the Library section offers inside information about the Library of Congress' holdings and directions for using the Library.

Compton's Encyclopedia (ENCYCLOPEDIA)

Compton's Encyclopedia online includes more than 9 million words in 5,274 long articles and 29,322 concise articles. Your child can search the encyclopedia using either title words or keywords. Of course, choosing this second method will result in far more articles brought to your screen. Onscreen help includes guidance in choosing search words, tools for constructing search queries, and tips for saving and printing articles. If your kids are going to be using the encyclopedia regularly, print out these instructions.

We posed a research question for a hypothetical independent study project of herbivorous dinosaurs. In fewer than 10 minutes, we located four entries concerning the giant plant-eaters. Three of them were directly relevant to our project. They ranged from a general description of plant-eating vs. meat-eating dinosaurs, to a specific discussion of the bird-hipped dinosaurs. We learned about the bone structure of the bird-hipped beasts and explored speculations about why they didn't survive as long as some of their dinosaur cousins did.

AskERIC Online (ERIC) (T)

The Educational Resources Information Center (ERIC) can be a very useful resource for you, although only your older cybernauts will be interested in exploring here for themselves. ERIC is supported by the U.S. Department of Education and by the Office of Educational Research and Improvement. Through the ERIC system, you can obtain research summaries, bibliographies, reference and referral services, computer searches, and documents on many education-related issues. Through America Online, you can search ERIC databases, ask research questions on the message boards, and learn about ERIC products and publications.

Scientific American Online (SCIAM) (T)

Scientific American is the oldest continuously published magazine in America. America Online makes it available to the new generation of science students exploring online. They can read the latest issue or recent back issues. They can get news updates from SA journalists, and exchange messages on the Reader to Reader message board.

This is a service most appropriate for your oldest students. Scientific American Online is populated by serious scientists and students of science. If this describes your teen, you can feel good about turning him loose here. Yes, he could subscribe to the hardcopy magazine or read it at the library, but if he lives and breathes science, he'll love interacting with other people who do too.

Electronic Schoolhouse (ESH)

This is an electronic gathering place where teachers, students, and parents (particularly homeschooling parents) can meet to link their classes together in mutual projects. One example is Students Watching Over Our Planet Earth (SWOOPE). The project participants include students and teachers from SWOOPE, the Illinois Rivers Project, The Acid Rain Project (TARP-IT), and the West Virginia Space Grant Consortium's Outreach Program. For one month in 1994, students from across the country measured the precipitation in their areas and calculated its pH.

The purpose of SWOOPE's projects is to give students insight into how science really works by collecting data over an extended period of time, controlling variables that occur in the world outside the laboratory, and sharing their findings with students around the country.

Science is just one area of study in the Electronic

Schoolhouse. There are also programs for geography, social studies, writing, math, and history.

NEA Public Forum (NEA PUBLIC) (T)
We don't believe your kids will have any interest in visiting this forum, but we are including it because you might. This is the online site for the National Education Association. It is filled with all manner of resources for teachers. Many of these will be interesting to you in enriching your child's education. The message board is quite lively and provides parents with an insider's view of the issues currently facing American education.

Education Industry Connection (T)
This menu is available from the list that appears when you access the Education button on America Online's Main Menu. It has no keyword because it is not an online area so much as a listing of companies that produce educational software. Listings include information about the companies and descriptions of their educational software offerings. Many of these products are available from the companies' stores on America Online. Some of the listings include online support areas for the software products and teacher's message boards for discussing uses of the software in the classroom.

Educational Software (T)
You will find this menu listed right below the Education Industry Connection on the Education menu. It is a listing of collections of educational software developed by America Online's Computing and Software department. America Online claims to have the largest collection of educational software available on any commercial online service. You will find software for Apple II, Mac, and IBM PC computers. Software libraries include programs for elementary, secondary, and college students, and teacher's aides. Programs include everything from arcade-like math games to

flash cards, to spelling helpers. Download times and equipment requirements are listed for each files.

COMPUSERVE

Grolier's Academic American Encyclopedia (GROLIERS)

Grolier's Academic American Encyclopedia on CompuServe includes over 10 million words in over 33,000 articles. It is updated quarterly. The user's guide helps you learn to define your search terms, and it makes it easy to find your way through the encyclopedia.

We tried to locate the answer to our question about evergreen and deciduous trees. In reading the directions for using the encyclopedia, we found vegetation to be one of the standard information bits available to all searches about geographic locations. Within a few minutes, we knew that oak and hickory trees abound in Maryland and evergreens include the Virginia pine, the loblolly, and the pitch. Pretty easy after all.

Information Please Almanac (GENALMANAC)

CompuServe is also the online home of the Information Please Almanac (see Figure 5.6). This is your online quick reference for all of those little bits of information that are momentarily vitally important. If you're the kind of family that keeps a paperback copy of the Almanac in the bathroom (not that we know of any like that), you'll love this quick and ready access to information tidbits online.

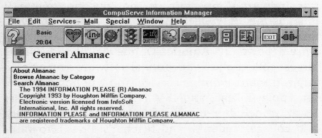

Figure 5.6 The Information Please Almanac

Kidnet

Categories of information covered include a concise guide to style for capitalization and punctuation guidance. Just about everything else from astronomy, to people, to world statistics is searchable in just a moment.

Knowledge Index (KI) ($) (T)

We generally don't recommend surcharged services for kids, especially database services. The cost is one issue, the skill necessary to search these databases is another. But if it's late at night and you really need that article or citation for a paper that's due tomorrow, these services cannot be beat.

Knowledge Index has long been one of the online industry's best bargains. It allows you to search through more than 100 publications; newspapers such as the Baltimore Sun; Books in Print; Historical Abstracts, and Computer Database are among the other files you can access. In many cases you can retrieve the full text of the article.

Knowledge Index is only available during these times:

Weekdays: Mon.–Thurs. 6:00 P.M. to 5:00 A.M.;
Weekends: Fri. 6:00 P.M. to Mon. 5:00 A.M.

It's priced at $24 per hour; there's no charge beyond this for retrieving the full text or abstracts of articles.

Education Forum (EDFORUM) (T)

The purpose of the Education Forum is to share information about all aspects of teaching and learning. It's a resource for teachers, parents, and to some extent students. You will be more likely to use it than your kids will.

If you're looking for educational software for your kids, you've found a great source. Library files abound. You can download a file to turn your PC into a microscope. Then download more files of slides to view on it! Software is available for helping your kids in math, geography, and science just to name a few. You will find puzzles and educational games.

Libraries also bulge with information from The International Society for Technology in Education, based in the University of Oregon. This group is working toward integrating technology into our nation's classrooms, and you'll find information about their programs and contests they sponsor.

Chuck Lynd, forum administrator, shared his educator's point of view about putting kids online. Although he said he could think of lots of reasons to encourage your kids online, he boiled them down to two. First, kids are so much quicker than grown-ups to pick up new ways and ideas. Teaching them to use online services now, makes this a "natural, second-nature means of communications for these kids, that will serve them throughout their lives." Secondly, he observed that all of America's educational philosophy is moving toward children taking ownership of their education and teachers becoming facilitators to that ownership. Online gives kids a way to ask any question and get it answered. Exposing them to this is exposing them to exactly the way they will be expected to learn in the future. Online gives teachers, parents, and kids the chance to individualize their curricula. If this kind of talk gets your blood flowing, stop into the Education Forum and say "Hi" to Chuck.

Science/Math Education Forum (SCIENCE) (T)

This is the place for CompuServe's users with a genuine interest in math and science. Your youngest children will be lost (just like your trusty guide was!), but some of your older kids will really be able to get help with their advanced math classes. If you have a budding scientist, she'll find kindred souls to communicate with here. We'll surely file this away for the future when our kids are in middle school and completely beyond getting help with math homework at home.

US News & World Report (USNEWS)

This fine news magazine is certainly not written for our audience, but its online version is colorful and attractive. If your child needs help with a current events assignment, you'll surely be able to track it down here. As an added bonus, this is part of CompuServe's basic services.

PRODIGY

Homework Helper (HH) ($)

Homework Helper is Prodigy's most impressive service offering for helping your kids with their schoolwork (see Figure 5.7). Homework Helper was designed and produced by Infonautics Corporation, an online services company that specializes in making information from a wide variety of sources easily accessible. For one year, Prodigy has an exclusive agreement with Infonautics, making Homework Helper available only through Prodigy. After that year is over, Homework Helper is likely to be available on other online services as well. Homework Helper premiered in February 1995 to much hype and hoopla in the press. Some of that excitement was well deserved.

Homework Helper is essentially a full-text database of material from more than 1,500 books, 500 magazines, and 100 newspapers. It also includes 1,500

Figure 5.7 Homework Helper Welcome Screen on Prodigy

photos and 300 maps. It is updated daily. Although it was designed for 10- to 19-year-old-kids, we think that older kids and adults will find it useful, too.

The difference between Homework Helper and other databases you'll find online is the search engine that makes the information easy to find. Instead of using keywords to create effective search phrases, you are encouraged to merely ask Homework Helper a question. You can select the sources of information you want to search, choose the subjects you want to search (e.g. history, sports, arts), and select how current you want the information to be. Then press a button and the search begins (see Figure 5.8).

To make your search more specific, you can store information about your child that Homework Helper will use every time it searches the database. This information includes your child's age, grade in school, hobbies, and favorite magazines.

Because Prodigy and Infonautics both bragged about asking Homework Helper open-ended questions and getting them answered, we decided to give it a try. We've been searching databases for a long time, and we know that when you are searching full-text articles, chances are good that you will get lots of results that aren't relevant to your search. To test Homework Helper, we decided to ask a question that Prodigy touted in its press release about the new service.

We asked, "What is the smartest animal?" We got 29 responses, rated for their relevance from 99 through 95. Of the 9 items rated at 99, none of them told us which animal is the smartest. We saw stories about smart animals, which was the portion of the question used as a search phrase. We read about which breeds of the dog family are thought to be smartest. We read about how smart pigs are. We also read of a storybook written by homeless children in which a smart animal (a bear) becomes lost and homeless. But none of these articles mentioned dolphins or apes, two species known for their intelligence, and none actually answered the question, "What is the Smartest Animal?"

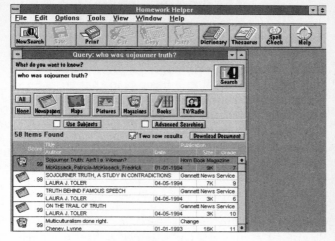

Figure 5.8 Homework Helper Search Screen on Prodigy

We tried again with a more direct, less open-ended question. This time we searched for information about Sojourner Truth, by asking the question, "Who was Sojourner Truth?" Ahhh, that's more like it! We found 52 items that included a book review of her biography, an entry from Compton's encyclopedia, stories from newspaper articles, and an archive photo of the lady herself. The search took only a few minutes from the 2 hours of time allotted for the month, and it provided ample research to complete our hypothetical report.

It is certainly wonderful that your child has access to a database that is searchable through simple questions. It is much better for him to be able to type, "Who was Sojourner Truth?" than it is to have to teach him "Sojourner" and "Truth" and "American" and "History." The value and usefulness of Homework Helper cannot be discounted. But, think about the information you need before you turn to a database that carries a premium price. If you want specifics about someone like Sojourner Truth, this is fabulous. It won't be as useful for your child if she needs to

99

know about John Kennedy. That subject is too vast for this type of a database search to be useful. She would get a more direct answer from an online encyclopedia that doesn't carry additional surcharges.

Homework Helper charges apply in one of two ways. You can enroll in a basic plan that costs $9.95 per month and includes 2 hours of searching. Time beyond those 2 hours is charged at a rate of $2.95 per hour. You can also choose a pay-per-view plan which is billed at a rate of $6.00 per hour with no minimum payment. These charges are in addition to the standard Prodigy fees.

To use Homework Helper, you must have Windows 3.1 and Prodigy software for Windows. You should also use a modem speed of 9600 bps or more. You can download the Homework Helper software directly from Prodigy when you jump to Homework Helper.

National Geographic Society (NATIONAL GEOGRAPHIC)

Prodigy offers a colorful weekly feature from the National Geographic Society (see Figure 5.9). Each week you will find a new quiz-based learning game.

Figure 5.9 National Geographic Society Screen on Prodigy

This week's quiz, for example, might be about whales and their migration. Your child is prompted to answer a series of questions. At each question, she can choose to investigate, reading information about whales that will lead her to the right answer. Each question she answers correctly reveals another portion of the picture of a whale, until the complete image is visible.

NOVA: (NOVA)

Produced by WGBH in Boston, each month the online Nova feature takes you on an entertaining adventure that explains a little about the universe (see Figure 5.10). When we first stopped in, Nova was featuring Operation Flustorm!—a clever graphic trip through the immune system of a young flu sufferer. Your commanding officer throughout the campaign was General Worstcough. (Okay, some of the jokes and puns are corny, but it's an entertaining and educational stop for your kids, anyway.)

The Nova area also features Beyond Belief: a biweekly column by NOVA columnist Ethan Her-

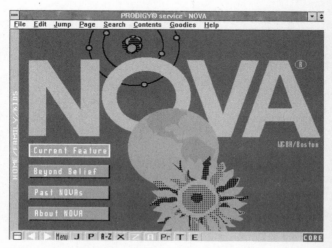

Figure 5.10 NOVA Screen on Prodigy

berman. Each Tuesday and Friday, Herberman presents the latest Beyond Belief column during which he offers explanations about why things are. Recent examples include a discussion of the structure of raccoon paws, and how that structure allows raccoons to do all sorts of things we don't want them to do. The column went on to explain why the raccoon population has grown so large in suburban America. Your child can ask Herberman scientific questions that he then uses in preparing future columns.

Education BB (EDUCATION BB) (Plus)
This is Prodigy's online message area for teachers and parents. Stop in here to discuss issues relating to your child's education with teachers, parents, and homeschoolers.

Grolier's Academic American Encyclopedia (ENCYCLOPEDIA)
Like CompuServe, Prodigy offers an online version of the Academic American Encyclopedia as part of its core service. See the description of the encyclopedia listed above.

Schoolware (SCHOOLWARE)
This is a list of the top ten software programs and CD-ROMs of interest to kids and schools. Each program rating includes a description of the product and current pricing information.

THE INTERNET

The World Wide Web
Using the Internet may not make homework fun, but it can certainly help your kids finish it faster; that is, unless they spend too much time "surfing." But with all the great stuff that's available, who could blame them?

Library of Congress World Wide Web Home Page
(http://lcweb.loc.gov/homepage/lchp.html)

This site has a lot of information about the Library of Congress' collections. There are also a number of electronic exhibits. We found the following when we stopped by:

The Gettysburg Address
The Russian Church and Native Alaskan Cultures
1492: An Ongoing Voyage
African American Culture and History
Scrolls from the Dead Sea

The exhibits included quite a bit of text, but also photographs, including some of lithographs. In time this will be a tremendous resource, but for now, the photographs we downloaded were not worth the wait—at least not at 14.4 bps.

As part of the American Memory collection, browsers can see primary source and archival material from American culture and history collections. All this is part of the growing national digital library, which will eventually bring these treasures, which belong to all of us, to everyone with access to a computer and modem.

The LOCIS (Library of Congress Information System) may be the best part of this site. This lets you search the electronic card catalog of one of the world's great libraries by subject or author. The system is fast, it provides access to information about millions of books, but it's not very pretty. Your kids may need some help in doing their first couple of searches.

Your next stop can be another site supported by your tax dollars, THOMAS.

THOMAS
(http://thomas.loc.gov/)
The US Congress' THOMAS site received a lot of attention when it first opened, and for good reason (see Figure 5.11). From here you can retrieve the full text of all House and Senate bills from the 103rd and 104th Congress, by keyword or bill number. Kids can

read articles such as "How Our Laws Are Made." They can also get to the Senate and House gophers, which by themselves include loads of resources such as the email addresses for senators and representatives. The site also includes educational materials such as the full text of the Constitution of the United States.

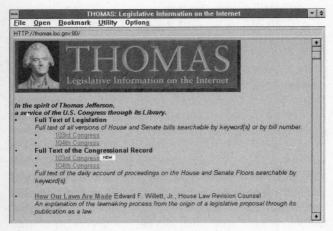

Figure 5.11 THOMAS WWW Home Page from the U.S. Congress

The Frog Dissection Page
(http://curry.eduschool.Virginia.EDU/~insttech/frog/)

In Chapter 13, we'll show you some frogs on ice. If you wonder what they look like on the inside, stop by here (see Figure 5.12). Kids love this frog dissection page, and we think it's pretty cool, too. The Frog Dissection Page shows you an interactive frog dissection, in parts, if you will. This page was meant for high school biology classes, but why should they have all the fun?

Views of the Solar System
(http://www.c3.lanl.gov/~cjhamil/SolarSystem/homepage.html)

As kids, we were fascinated by the solar system—the sheer vastness of it, the tremendous distances

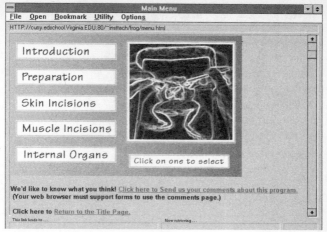

Figure 5.12 Frog Dissection WWW Home Page

involved, the size of Jupiter, the rings of Saturn, the heat of the Sun, and, oh yes, our own planet Earth. Stop here for a great educational tour of the Sun, planets, moons, asteroids, comets, and meteoroids (see Figure 5.13). Click on a planet, for example, and related images and information appears—enough for any school report. You may also find links for the planets' moons. The image files are large, so remind your 8- to 14-year-olds to be patient.

Academy One
(http://www.nptn.org/cyber.serv/AOneP/)

Academy One is the educational arm of the National Public Telecommunications Network (see Appendix B). It was started by Linda Delzeit who had her two daughters in mind at the time. Linda feels that "raw Internet" and kids don't mix. The idea behind Academy One was to build a place where "students are safe and can experiment, share, learn, and do curriculum-oriented projects from home or school."

Through this very kid-friendly service kids can tap into simulation projects, science and foreign language projects, a TeleOlympics, and our favorite, a

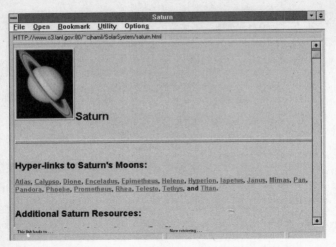

Figure 5.13 Views of the Solar System WWW Home Page

Spotlight on People section. Here students write and ask questions of prominent leaders, inventors, authors, and professionals. To get things started, the accomplished individual contributes a biography.

Parents: Academy One was specifically designed for new users, so everyone can feel comfortable here. There's even a Parents are Teachers section for parents to connect with one another.

Peterson's Education Center
(http://www.petersons.com:8080/) (T)

Peterson's has been helping students make intelligent decisions about which colleges and universities to apply to for years. This site was just getting underway when we checked. The Summer Programs section was already completed. Kids can stop here to read about summer programs available from 1400 organizations, from camps to tour groups. Search alphabetically or geographically. Travel and sports camps are included!

General career information and advice was scheduled to be a part of the site. All in all, kids will find a lot of the information is for older students, such as details about undergraduate colleges and graduate programs. Clearly this is a site your kids can grow with.

EdWeb
(http://k12.cnidr.org:90/resource.cntnts.html) (T)
Primarily a site for educators, parents should take a look at the link for The Educational Resource Guide. From this page, kids and parents can get to a tremendous number of links and educational resources on the Net in these categories:

- Information Services: Gopher and the World Wide Web
- Private Discussion Groups and Electronic Journals
- Public Discussion Groups and News Services
- Commercial Collaborative Learning Services
- Chat Forums for Kids
- Educational Gateways
- General Educational Networks
- State-Sponsored Educational Networks
- Question & Answer Services

Educational Online Sources
(http://netspace.students.brown.edu/eos/main–image. html) (T)
This site is more for parents than kids. We include it because we are going to assume you are new to the Internet and could benefit from the ample resources that have been pulled together here. Its focus is on how the Internet can aid education. There are links to Internet guides, education-related newsgroups, and Web sites of interest to parents and educators.

Web 66 (What's New)
(http://web66.coled.umn.edu/new/new.html)
Web 66 is the place to go on the Internet if your child's school is looking for help in creating its own Web site. The Web 66 site includes this page of links

to "home pages or other WWW projects by and for kids." The emphasis is on the academic—sites at schools, in particular.

Newsgroups

We feel students are better served by the Web sites and associated gophers when researching school assignments, than they are by newsgroups. Newsgroups may not provide information in a timely fashion. When you have an assignment, you may not be able to wait until someone answers your newsgroup posting.

Of course, if you are working on a long-term assignment, you may be able to wait for an answer to your posting. In that case, we recommend searching for an appropriate newsgroup, using your online service provider's Search All Newsgroups (or the equivalent) feature.

A book report on the southwest, for example, could be enhanced by the answers to a few well-phrased queries posed on the alt.culture.us.southwest newsgroup. As we've said before, not that many kids use newsgroups right now, so it's important to read the FAQs associated with them, lurk for a while to get the tone of the newsgroup down, and pose well-thought-out questions. Despite the few exceptions you may have read about in newspaper or magazine accounts, there are many helpful people on the Net who enjoy helping others out.

THE BEST OF THE REST

eWorld

Blackberry Creek: Kids Creativity Community (BLACKBERRY)
From this attractively laid-out place, kids can "put on a play, plan a party, create their own books, and have fun with other creative computer users" (see Figure 5.14). When you come here, read past issues of the Blackberry Creek Gazette to get a feel for what goes on. Kids come here to write and share stories and plays. For

example, the winner of a recent pet story contest submitted a story about his "pet" dragon, David. David is a million years old and a planteater. Kids could download the complete story and even a picture of David. The winner won a copy of KidPix 2, so now he can draw more pictures of his friends.

Through Story Weaver, a live story writing activity, everybody works together to collaborate on a story. Check out the Story Weaver folder within Creekside Publishing for past stories.

Here are the places in Blackberry Creek that your kids can click on to visit:

- Blackberry Creek Gazette (A newspaper)
- Kids Hangout (A BBS/Forum)
- Parents Club (A BBS/Forum)
- What's Happening (A calendar of events)
- The Hungry Ear (A live-chat center)
- Little Theater (A center for performing artists and entertainers)
- Creekside Publishing (A spot for aspiring journalists)
- Party and Gift Shop (A place to plan parties and create gifts with your computer)
- The Exchange (Where files are stored)

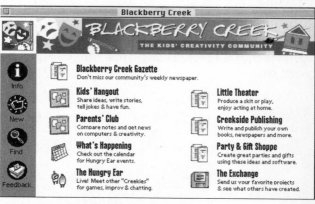

Figure 5.14 Blackberry Creek on eWorld

TimeMachine (TIME MACHINE)

This is a searchable database of information about events in the past, including "articles, image, sound, and movie files." It needs to be filled out. Under biographies, in one of the libraries, we only found three people featured, Benjamin Franklin, Frederick Douglass, and Booker T. Washington.

GEnie

Space and Science Round Table (SPACERT)

Here's a spot on GEnie to drop in for help with math and science. There is a help desk set up for students of all ages who need help in these areas.

Writers' Ink Round Table (WRITERS)

Kids can come here for helpful, specific advice about getting their work published. We learned, for example, about a book called Kathy Henerson's Youth's Guide to Markets. It turns out she contributes to the forum occasionally and tends to pop into the Submission Advice for Young Writers section.

Computer Assisted Learning Center (CALC) Online Campus (CALC)

CALC Online Campus is an international online tutoring and course center. Students of all ages can come here to take courses, get tutoring and homework help, discover projects to reinforce lessons, and get information about colleges and universities. Subjects covered include English, math, science, and social studies.

TV and Movies

"Turn it off! Turn it off! I can't stand hearing it any-more." Parents all over the country have been known to echo this cry. It's impossible to be a parent in the 1990s and not wonder what effect TV is having on our kids. But, what if you could turn the TV from a passive time thief into an interactive medium; a tool that kids can use and control? When you combine TV with online services, you bring about profound changes in the way kids consume TV and the movies. Kids and their parents now have direct access to the executives who bring us our favorite shows and movies. We can take an active role in seeing to it that we get what we want. Online you will find not only other fans who want to talk about your favorites, but also areas created by the networks and studios so that you can sound off about what you're viewing. Network staff members are regular online users, and they want your opinion. If you like it, tell them. If you don't like it, tell them now!

Figure 6.1 A movie director for the Cyberspace Age

ABC Classroom (ABC CLASSROOM)

ABC designed this online area for teachers who use ABC programming in their classrooms. The service provides program previews and information about using ABC shows to teach. You will also find back issues of ABC Classroom Connection, the quarterly magazine for teachers.

Many of the features of ABC Classroom are geared toward teachers. Many others look more like advertisements for ABC than any classroom we've ever visited. Still, there are some activities that your kids may be interested in checking out.

The ABC Auditorium is the site for live chats with ABC guest speakers. A standard feature of the Auditorium is Careers For Kids! This is a weekly conference featuring professionals from all walks of life. During the conferences, kids are welcome to ask questions of the guest expert. The week we visited, an oceanographer and marine science researcher was available. Other guests include kids' TV personalities from ABC and other networks, too.

Your kids may also find the ABCNews Library to be useful. Here they will find text and graphic images that include transcripts and biographies, maps and video clips.

Transcripts include the American Agenda, Person of the Week, Peter Jennings' Journal Radio Commentary, and ABC news Polling results. There are map collections from countries and cities all over the world and a collection of international flags. The tools your kids will need to download and view the files are also stored in the library.

Achievement TV (ACHIEVEMENT TV)

This site is an extension of the American Academy of Achievement's Salute to Excellence. It is meant to be used in conjunction with Achievement TV program-

Kidnet

ming. These programs are available to schools throughout the country, but they also reach 58 million homes through cable networks such as the Arts and Entertainment network.

Online, pre-broadcast lesson plans are free of charge, and prepared by the Encyclopaedia Britannica Educational Corporation. Achievement TV features guests who have made important contributions to life in the 20th Century. Kids can attend many of the teleconferences via the TV and an 800 number. The service holds monthly essay contests and awards prizes to conference attendees. Winning essayists receive a $250 savings bond, their schools win a 24-volume set of Britannica's *The Annals of America*, and the winning essays are featured on America Online. This service is geared mostly toward educators and the high schoolers they teach.

Kids Only Star Trek Club (KIDS)

When we were working on this book, the Kids Only Star Trek Club was under construction. Until that construction is complete, you will find an active Star Trek forum (STARTREK) available on America Online; it just isn't specifically meant for kids. In the Kids Only area, you will find some crossover files, such as conference schedules and library files (in this case called Record Banks). No doubt, by the time you read this, the Star Trek Club in the Kids Only area will be complete, and your little Trekkies will have a home of their own on America Online.

Disney Adventure Magazine (DISNEY)

More than 5 million kids read Disney Adventure magazine every month. America Online subscribers can come here to suggest story ideas and chat with the editors (see Figure 6.2). They can also check out what's coming up in future features. The Odeon Auditorium is for live conferences. The message boards include a folder for celebrity information and addresses. Kids post messages with screen names and online addresses of their favorite stars. Whether or not these are accurate remains to be seen, but the kids love talking about their favorite shows and stars. When we checked out the Cool Fads folder, we learned that POGS are cool. We already knew that

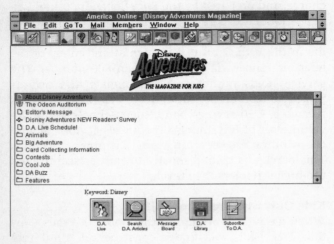

from looking at our kitchen table!

Figure 6.2 Disney Adventure Magazine Screen on America Online

Walt Disney World Resort (DISNEY)

Whether you're planning a trip to Disney World, you want to relive your vacation, or you just want to dream a little, drop into the Walt Disney World Resort (see Figure 6.3). This colorful tour of Disney World is full of information about park schedules, special shows, rides, and resort features (see Figure 6.4). It's lively and fun for kids to browse. Parents will be interested in the practical information about tickets, package tours, and accommodations. You'll also find a message board folder, Disney Vets Help Newcomers. Here you'll find advice from folks who have been there often about the best way to plan your trip.

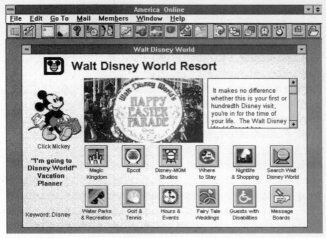

Figure 6.3 Walt Disney World Resort on America Online

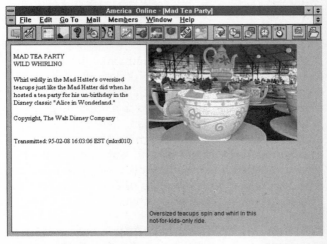

Figure 6.4 Mad Tea Party Wild Whirling Ride from Walt Disney World on America Online

Discovery Channel (DISCOVERY)

The Discovery Channel was a founding member of the Cable in the Classroom program. Every day it offers 18 hours of non-fiction broadcasting about nature and the environment, science and technology, history and social studies. The Discovery Channel Online includes information about upcoming shows and schedules, downloadable .GIFs from shows already aired, and message boards for exchanging ideas about Discovery Channel programs.

You will also find The Discovery Channel Education Area. This is a resource for teachers who use the documentaries that form Assignment Discovery in their classrooms, but there is plenty of useful information for parents and kids here too. For each documentary featured, you will find mini-lesson plans, questions and answers, and vocabulary lists. You and your child can use these in viewing the Discovery Channel programming to expand the educational value of the documentaries. All right, your kids would rather hang out at MTV Online, but you'll be delighted by the high-quality material that you'll find in the Discovery Channel Online.

The Learning Channel (TLC)

The Learning Channel was launched by Discovery Network in 1991 for preschool kids and older. Don't be deceived by the preschool classification. You'll find plenty of material here for your elementary school kids and even some information that would relate to your high schoolers. The Learning Channel explores humanities, arts, sciences, and entertainment. It is structured just like the Discovery Channel Online, with message boards, libraries of downloadable files, and conference areas for live chats.

Sci-Fi Channel (SCIFI CHANNEL)

If your kids love watching the Sci-Fi Channel, they'll be happy to spend some time here (see Figure 6.5). The FTL (Faster Than Light) Newsfeed is an ongoing news report from the future. The Fan Dome is the online chat area where science fiction lovers can gather for real-time discussions and visits with guests. The Lab is the message area where your kids can interact with the executives at the Sci Fi Channel and other sci-fi fans.

Kidnet

Finally, the Graphic Inter-Mission area is the store-house of downloadable files. Your kids will find programming schedules, descriptions of upcoming shows, and promotions of upcoming specials. The Inside Space report includes news about space exploration and attempts to contact alien life forms. The Search the Online Area feature allows you to enter keywords and search the program schedules for your favorite shows, writers, or stars of science fiction.

Figure 6.5 Sci-Fi Channel on America Online

MTV Online (MTV) (T)

MTV presents a dilemma for lots of parents. When are kids old enough to watch the network, enjoy the music, and not be unduly influenced by some of its attitude? If you've answered this question, and you're comfortable with your kids watching MTV, they'll want to stop by MTV Online and check it out. There is lots of news here about the music industry, and lots of information about the TV network too. Your kids will find birthday listings for their favorite groups and stars and lots of fan clubs they can join. The Bio-rythms area stores biographic information about performers. Your kids will find lots of images for downloading in the Eye Candy area. The MTV Online message boards reflect the attitude of the MTV network. We strongly suggest you visit here first to decide if this spot meets with your approval for your kids. They'll probably love it, but you may not.

E! Entertainment Television (E!)

E! is the online spot for the cable network E! Entertainment Television. Although you'd think this would be a great place for kids who love entertainment, you'd be surprised. When we explored it, this area was almost laughably out-dated. For example, on the first day of Spring, the new "Hot Off the Presses" area included a news story dated January 11! Not exactly hot stuff! The area also included Casey Kasem's Top 10 list, also two months old. Save your online time and money until these folks can keep the service up to date.

COMPUSERVE

All-Movie Guide (ALLMOVIE) (T)

Your youngest kids won't be interested in this feature, but you can use it to check out movies and videos they want to see. Your older kids, if they're really into movies, will find it easy to use and very useful. The All-Movie Guide is a searchable database of more than 50,000 documents. You can search the database by title, actor/actress, ratings, or type of movie. If your kids follow the career of a particular star, they can get a history of every movie that star has made. You won't find listings for the most current releases, but this is a great place to stop off before you head to the video store.

Entertainment Drive (EDRIVE) (T)

The EDrive calls itself "your backstage pass to the entertainment industry." Through the EDrive your kids can interact with industry professionals from the world of TV, movies, and theater. Networks, studios, and producers submit both articles and photos to the EDrive libraries. Your kids will also find polls

Kidnet

and member's choice awards, .WAV and .GIF files for downloading. Remember that this forum is not expressly meant for children. For example, some of the .GIF files are mature in nature. If your kids are really into the entertainment industry, accompany them to the EDrive. Because this proved to be so popular with kids, CompuServe and the EDrive staff members developed the YDrive, specifically for young people. Your kids, especially your youngest cybernauts, will be better off exploring there instead.

YDrive (YDRIVE)

Late in 1994, the YDrive came online as a place where kids can pursue their entertainment interests in a safe, well supervised environment (see Figure 6.6). It is the link between kids and the folks who produce their entertainment. Here, your kids can interact with other kids, entertainment executives, and stars of their favorite shows. Early in 1995, for example, the YDrive hosted a live chat with the kids from CBS's hit *The Nanny*. Members of the cast of *Party of Five* on Fox have stopped by on the message board to exchange messages with forum members.

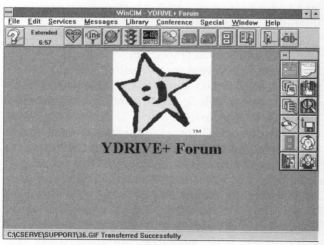

Figure 6.6 CompuServe's YDrive Welcome Screen

119

The YDrive was also the first CompuServe forum to allow kids to be members of the forum staff. Kids are section leaders on the message boards, and help the forum administrators create and maintain the content of the forum. The philosophy here is that kids are smart, savvy people. They know what they want, and they should have the opportunity to let the grown-ups in charge know about it, too. On top of all of this, the forum is staffed by a group of adults who are both knowledgeable about the online world and dedicated to creating a safe community where kids can express themselves freely. Send your kids into the YDrive for plenty of entertainment fun, and you won't have to worry about what they'll find here or who they'll meet.

EDrive Movie Forum (EMOVIES)

This forum is different from the usual CompuServe forum in that it doesn't contain any message boards. Instead it is a library of files that include full-motion video and stereo audio clips of actual movie scenes. Your kids can come here to download biographies of their favorite stars, complete with photos. They will also find information about what's coming next from the major movie studios.

The TV Zone Forum (TVZONE)

The difference between this forum and the others we've already talked about is that this one is dedicated strictly to television. It is not a kids' offering, but any kid who loves TV will find plenty of interesting stuff here. There is a message section hosted by Joe Adalian, the TV writer/critic for the New York Post. There are message sections devoted to sitcoms, dramas, soap operas, even TV commercials! We think you begin to get the idea.

Roger Ebert's Movie Reviews (EBERT)

If you've got a kid who likes the show Sneak Previews, you've got a kid who'll like Ebert's online home. It is filled with reviews of recent and not so recent movies. It's easy to search the database for a movie you're interested in or for your favorite movie stars. There are also essays submitted by Roger and interviews with celebrities. This is a favorite online spot for us. Will your kids want to come here? Maybe, if they're really into movies. It's more likely, though, that you'll use it to check out the movies they want to go see.

Hollywood Hotline tm (HHL)
This fun spot offers a wide variety of entertainment features, from TV and movie reviews to headlines to celebrity interviews.

The Entertainment Encyclopedia is filled with information, and it's fun to use. Your kids can check out celebrity birthdays, winners of past Academy Awards, Grammy and Tony Awards, or they can follow the Beatles tour history. Snippets of entertainment trivia that may be hard to find in other places are just waiting for you here at Hollywood Hotline.

Magill's Survey of Cinema (MAGILL) ($)
This database includes articles about more than 30,000 films released since 1902. Although it is a fine source of information for movie buffs, it is also a surcharged service. Charges accumulate for every search you conduct. For your children's purposes, have them stick with Roger Ebert's reviews for this sort of thing. They'll find everything they need there without the extra charge.

Hollywood Online Forum (FLICKS)
In the libraries of the Hollywood Online forum, your kids will find interactive multimedia "kits" including pictures and sounds from some of their favorite movies. When we checked, they could download kits from *Forrest Gump, Star Trek Generations, The Mask,* and *Dumb and Dumber,* just to name a few. These kits feature a snippet of footage from the film and little else

of value. They're large files, so they take a long time to download. You may find better uses for your online dollar. Movie buffs of every variety abound on the message board and in the conference areas, but your kids would be more likely to find their peers in the YDrive.

Showbizmedia Forum (SHOWBIZ)

The Showbizmedia forum is run by the same folks who bring you the TV Zone forum. It covers all forms of show business including movies, TV, radio, and the stage. Roger Ebert has his own message section, and so does Joe Bob Briggs from Joe Bob's Drive-In Theater. The libraries include hundreds of .GIFs of favorite stars and starlets, both current and classic. Your kids can also find Windows and Mac versions of video, sound, and pictures from recent movies.

Archive Films+ Forum (ARCFILM) (T)

This forum is a very serious place and your kids would only come here to use the libraries. The libraries hold more than 14,000 hours of footage drawn from newsreels, silent films, classical comedies, Hollywood features, historical dramas, documentaries, vintage educational and industrial films. We took a trip through the library under the heading Famous Faces. We found images of Franklin Roosevelt from the 1940s and Richard Nixon from the 1950s. The Hollywood Stars section included Greta Garbo, Marilyn Monroe, and Atlantic City Beauty Pageant contestants from the 1920s. We're not saying your kids won't be interested, but we're not betting the mortgage money this month either.

PRODIGY

Prodigy gives you a TV hot button on the Entertainment menu. Pressing that button takes you to the TV main menu where your choices are plain to see.

Much of what we found on Prodigy qualifies as online advertisements for different networks. Yes, if your kids have a favorite show on a particular network, they'll likely find a spot on Prodigy to talk about it with other fans, but they'll also wade through a lot of network hype to get there. We've included a list of the networks that keep online spots on Prodigy to make it easy for you to see what's available. When you go onto Prodigy, press the Networks Online hot button from the TV main screen for an update.

NETWORKS ONLINE WITH PRODIGY

Bravo	Family Channel
Cartoon Network	HBO
CBS	Learning Channel
NBC	Mind Extension U
Comedy Central	The Movie Channel
Country Music TV	Sci-Fi Channel
Disney Channel	USA Network
Discovery	

Total TV Online
Under this hot button, your kids will find weekly feature stories about the world of TV. They will also find TV listings, schedules, and reviews of upcoming shows.

Today's TV
This is a program listing of what's on TV today. Sure, if your kids happen to be on Prodigy anyway when they realize they meant to check out a listing, they can hop right over and do the job. On the other hand, the daily newspaper also includes this information, and you don't have to pay connect time charges while your kids read it.

U-to-U (UTOU)

U-to-U is an example of what happens when people integrate the online medium with the broadcast medium. Kids go online in the U-to-U area of Prodigy and interact with the people who produce this Nickelodeon show (see Figure 6.7). Via Prodigy, kids connect with other kids from around the world, and they all connect with Nickelodeon. Check out the Subject lists on the bulletin board and look for U-Mail letters from the show's staff members. Answer them, and watch U-to-U on Nickelodeon to see hosts Ali Rivera and Sertrone Starks log onto Prodigy and read kids' messages on TV. Your kids can also send email to the board leaders with their ideas for the show. They are active participants in creating the program they watch.

Each week, U-to-U also conducts an opinion poll. Here's an example. If you could have $1,000, and all you had to do to get it was to eat a bowl of ants, would you do it? The poll results are available online, or you can get them when you watch U-to-U. Time spent taking the polls and reading the results is free

Figure 6.7 Nickelodeon's U-to-U on Prodigy

Kidnet

of connect time charges. Time spent on the bulletin boards or in sending email to the staff of U-to-U is charged at Prodigy's Plus rates.

The Big Help (BIG HELP)
In the Fall of 1994, Nickelodeon sponsored The Big Help. This was an ongoing program designed to get kids interested in volunteering in their hometowns to help repair the world. Online, kids can check out the message boards (a Plus service) to see what other kids are doing to clean up their parts of the world. They're doing a lot! You'll find kids who are staffing homeless shelters, working with the elderly, and raising funds for all types of charity work. The message boards are filled with notes that begin, "I only pledged 3 hours, but now I'm working 4 hours a week..." Kids come online to talk about what they're doing and how it makes them feel. These kids are devoted to volunteerism, and they are establishing volunteer habits that they believe will last their lifetimes.

Ongoing polls show kids how others are volunteering and ask kids their opinions about different subjects. For example, Do animals get enough help from humans? The results indicated that 82 percent of the kids who responded thought that animals do not. The feeling was the same for both genders, throughout all regions of the country, and across all age groups. The results of the polls are updated instantly so you can see the most current outcome of your vote. Taking the polls and reviewing the results are free of connect time charges.

Out of Our Minds (OUT OF OUR MINDS)
This is Prodigy's weekly poll site to find out what your kids think about the latest in TV, movies, politics and more (see Figure 6.8). Each Friday a new poll starts. At the end of the week, the results are tabulated and put up for viewing. Your kids can vote as many times as they wish. Out of Our Minds is linked

to the Teen bulletin board and the Club bulletin board for kids up to 13. Kids can feel free to go on the bulletin boards and make their cases for their points of view. If they're good enough, they can persuade a bunch of other kids to vote with them and control the outcome of this week's poll. It's the American Way!!!

Figure 6.8 Prodigy's Out of Our Minds Poll Screen

THE INTERNET

The World Wide Web

As with the commercial services, there are a lot of elaborate "commercials" on the Internet from television networks, movie studios, and other entertainment meccas. We steer clear of those unless the site also offers a lot of other worthwhile information for fans. After all, there's nothing quite like a young fan, is there?

It's likely that you will find more than one site devoted to a popular television show or movie. For example, the Simpsons, at this writing, had more than six sites devoted to them, including one that

Kidnet

originated in Finland. In this case, how do you find the best? One option is to check out all six, or however many there are. Or, if there's also a newsgroup devoted to the topic (for the Simpsons it's .alt.tv.simpsons), post a message there and ask for opinions.

As you might expect, it's common to find a lot of sounds, graphics, and even video as part of Web sites devoted to TV and movies. For example, from the Beavis Web page you can download scores of "cool sounds" such as "hehe" "life sucks" "shut up!" It's not our taste, but lots of kids do like it.

The Power Rangers' Homepage
(http://kilp.media.mit.edu:8001/power/homepage.html)

This is a great place for kids to quench their perennial thirsts for information on the Power Rangers (see Figure 6.9). There are Power Ranger FAQs and episode guides, a Power Rangers toy list, a full picture database, and a monster gallery. Kids can also get the latest on the Power Rangers movie.

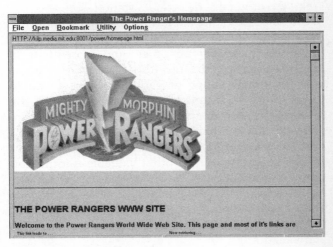

Figure 6.9 Power Rangers' Home Page

Webmaster Manny Perez feels the actor pages are the site's best features. There your kids can click on the characters and watch them morph into their Power Ranger forms, or back into just regular teens. We tried it for ourselves and thought it was pretty cool. "You can also click on various hypertext items and see their zords," Manny says. (We guess that's good.) Manny specifically asked us to encourage kids to write to him about what they'd like to see on the site.

Star Trek Resources on the Internet
(http://www.cosy.sbg.ac.at:/rec/startrek/star_trek_resources.html)
The amount of Star Trek-related information on the Internet is staggering. There are a lot of reasons for this, but mostly it's because the Net (i.e., Cyberspace) and the idea behind a show like Star Trek just seem to go together.

A recent Purdue university study asked kids who was most important in their lives in promoting science. Kids claimed it was the characters from Star Trek—the original series and its spinoff.

The place to start exploring the final frontier on the Internet is the Star Trek resources page, which has links to newsgroups, files, and more than 30 StarTrek–related Web sites. It's not very pretty but it does an excellent job of gathering links to all of these resources in one place. Alas, a couple of the newsgroups seemed marginal for kids (alt.sex.fetish.startrek; alt.sexy.bald.captains) and we wouldn't normally recommend this site for that reason, but there's simply too much other valuable information not to mention it.

The Star Wars Home Page
(http://stwing.resnet.upenn.edu:8001/~-jruspini/starwars.html)
While we're lost in space anyway, we thought we'd cover this site. This is definitely the place on the net

A long time ago in a galaxy far, far, away...

The Star Wars Home Page

This page has just undergone a major overhaul. It's now more modular: use the main menu to make sure you don't miss anything. Please excuse any minor ongoing construction.

This link leads to . . .   Now retrieving . . .

Figure 6.10 Star Wars Home Page

for Star Wars fans (see Figure 6.10). Look here for the latest news about the "Star Wars galaxy" and lots of articles about Star Wars collectibles.

The Lion King
(http://bvp.wdp.com/BVPM/PRessroom/LionKing/Lion King.html)
This is a favorite of many kids, but we can only rec-ommend it if you have a fast modem and a patient child. It's loaded with graphics and movie clips, which can take a long time to download. Some of the graphic files are under 50,000 bytes, and with a speedy modem you can pull those down at under 30 seconds.

Fox Broadcasting
(http://www.eden.com/users/my-html/fox.html)
This is a page of links to web sites for Fox shows. These include such kid favorites as Animaniacs, Batman: The Animated Series, and The Simpsons.

Newsgroups
There are over 100 Internet newsgroups devoted to discussions of television shows and movies, including

those that attract kids. Examples of topics covered include:

- Barney
- Beavis-N-Butthead
- Nickelodeon (in general)
- "Monster" movies
- "Cult" movies
- MTV

Because of the postings that may show up, we would generally not recommend these for kids. Some are quite busy (Animaniacs); others have surprisingly little traffic. Even the ones that would seem to be innocuous may feature language you wouldn't want your kids to see. For example, we found posted on the Brady Bunch newsgroup a nasty little ditty about "fags" that was a takeoff on the show's theme song. The writer was roundly flamed, but the damage had been done. On a commercial service that message would have been deleted; the author may have lost his forum privileges.

There are better places for kids to chat about their favorite TV shows and stars online than Internet newsgroups. These include forums on the commercial services simply because someone monitors them.

THE BEST OF THE REST

Delphi
FOXtalk
Delphi has an exclusive arrangement with the Fox network. Kids can stop in here to leave messages with Fox executives and discuss their favorite Fox shows on message boards and in live conferences. As of this writing, Delphi's interface is still text-only, so your kids won't think this is pretty. Delphi has promised a new interface by the end of 1995, so as you read this, it may look much better.

eWorld

Hollywood Online (HOLLYWOOD)

This is basically a public relations outlet for Hollywood. If your kids are looking for photos, film clips, or information from recent films, they'll find it here. An interesting section called Movie Notes includes the usual star bios, but through here your kids can also retrieve production notes from films. These include the actual Hollywood-issued plot summaries for recent movies.

7 ••••••••••••  •••••••••••••••

Music

Remember 16 Magazine? Forget about it! If your kids are into music, they'll discover a fascinating world of music fun and activity online that we once only dreamed about. Music and the online world are coming together to create interactivity between artists and fans. As teenagers we followed news of our favorite groups, eagerly waited for the next album release, and hoped to find them interviewed in magazines such as "16." Some of us may have joined fan clubs or sent off fan mail, but we had no way to directly reach our favorite stars.

The online world brings music alive and into your home. Music is no longer something your kids just consume. They can interact with their favorite stars through message exchanges or live conferences. They can even attend concert extravaganzas just for onliners. In 1994, Aerosmith held a Cybertour on the Internet, America Online, CompuServe, and Prodigy. Fans gathered for a virtual concert, and at each location, the band accepted questions from their audiences. Your kids may or may not care about

Figure 7.1 The group Widespread Panic, Capricorn Records, downloaded from ABC Rock & Road (AOL). Courtesy of Dan Skolnik (Shmogger).

Aerosmith, but they'll have to agree that the same kind of experience with their favorite group would rule!

AMERICA ONLINE

Music Message Center (MMC)

This is a good place to come and jump into a music discussion. This message center is the central menu for America Online's message boards directed at every aspect of music, from classical to rap to heavy metal. On these boards, you find discussions of every topic imaginable. Your kids will immediately enter into discussions of their favorite musicians. People swap opinions, news, gossip, and tips about buying the latest releases or concert tickets.

SPIN Online (SPIN)

This online version of SPIN magazine is colorful, lively, and fun (see Figure 7.2). Your kids can stop in to mix and mingle with Rock stars, music writers, and the magazine's editors. They'll find online conferences to attend, sound clips and graphics to download, and contests to enter.

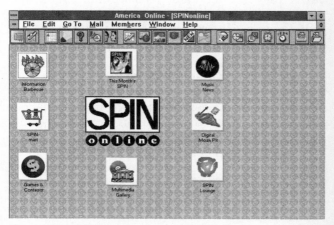

Figure 7.2 SPIN Online on America Online

The Mosh Pit is the center for live chats and message boards. The message boards are active and lively. Remember our warnings about live chats and kids. This area was designed for all Rock lovers, not just kids. A lot of the visitors are going to be older than your kids. That's not to say live chats should be off-limits, it's just a warning that you will want to accompany your kids to them and decide for yourself.

The SPIN Lounge is the site of weekly conferences with musicians, writers, and other SPIN readers. When we visited, SPIN editor and publisher Bob Guccione, Jr. was scheduled to speak about the magazine's 10th anniversary and what the first 10 years have seen.

RockLink™ Forum (ROCKLINK)

Rocklink™ Forum is America Online's own version of the RockNet information service. RockNet can also be found on other online services. RockLink information includes reports about the status of Rock and Roll today, information about all new vinyl and video releases, and accurate music charts and opinion polls. The information is updated daily.

Your kids can't come here for interactive chatting, but if they're after hard, reliable information and news, they'll find it. Columns include the Daily Beat, Rock News, Reviews/Charts/Concert Line, Gossip, and Rock Interviews.

Warner/Reprise Online (WARNER)

This is the online home of Warner/Reprise records. Your kids can come here looking for information about their favorite artists working on this record label. You'll find interviews with musicians. We read an interview with Eric Clapton who talked about his newest release, *From the Cradle*. He discussed its relevance to his other work, the roots of his inspiration, and what his smash album *Unplugged* has meant to him.

Not only Rock stars are here, but musicians of every flavor from jazz to rap to country and gospel. If the musician is signed to Warner/Reprise, you'll find information and a biography here.

This area is not just for gathering information. Your kids can exchange messages, participate in live chats, and download graphic and sound files. A complete tour schedule of Warner/Reprise artists is also here.

ABC Online Rock & Road (RR)

Rock & Road is a forum and a "point of focus" for the cyberspace lives of new Rock bands (see Figure 7.3). Each season, the forum focuses on about a dozen groups with strong followings among America Online members. These members join Rock & Road editors in following these bands and reporting from the road. Show reviews and tour schedules are just some of the information they share.

The forum message boards are for discussing bands, song lyrics, concerts, or whatever else members are thinking about. The forum libraries are available for people to share their listening experiences by uploading their favorite guitar riff or snippet of an artist interview. The forum also main-

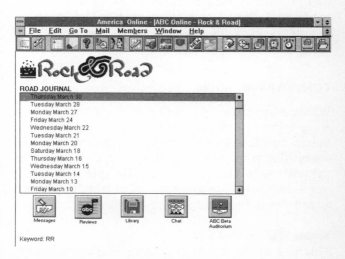

Figure 7.3 ABC Rock & Road on America Online

tains a database of concert information, including schedules and seating charts for the country's major concert locations.

Live chat areas allow forum members to talk in realtime with band members. The forum is hoping to sponsor an invitation-only rooftop concert with some of the bands they follow at the end of each season. Invitations will be extended to those forum members who regularly contribute to the fun.

Grateful Dead Forum (DEAD)

Hard as it may be to believe, some of the original Deadheads are grandparents now! That hasn't stopped a whole new generation of kids from discovering the Dead and carrying on the 30-year tradition of undying devotion to them. You'll find everything for Deadheads in the Grateful Dead Forum, from news to tour schedules, message boards to online chats. A long-standing and vibrant message thread was building when we were there. The discussion concerned the Generation Gap among Deadheads. Is it real? What could be causing it, and how is it different from the Generation Gap we parents remember? As if this weren't enough, the forum includes complete instructions for accessing Internet newsgroups and mailing lists about the Dead. Come hear Uncle John's Band.

COMPUSERVE

When Aerosmith took to CompuServe to release a song it was a PR bonanza for the group. Since then, countless groups have appeared online with everything from songs, to videos, to chat areas. As the virtual world became the hip place to hang out, musicians—always mindful of trends—started appearing in force.

Music Hall (MUSIC)

This is a great first stop in your search for music on CompuServe (see Figure 7.4). Recognizing how

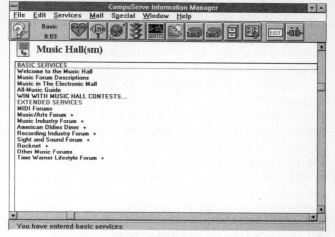

Figure 7.4 The Music Hall Screen on CompuServe

many users would be interested in music, CompuServe created this menu to direct you through the service to music offerings you may want to explore. You will find descriptions of all the music-related forums on CompuServe, including listings of their message board sections. You will also find listings of the music vendors in the Electronic Mall.

All-Music Guide (ALLMUSIC)

On CompuServe, the All-Music Guide (AMG) is a database collection of music albums, ratings, and reviews. Offline it is a 1,200-page book and a CD-ROM. The AMG represents the combined efforts of over 200 music writers who feature the most important artists and their best music. These reviewers include liner note writers, and writers from such famous magazines in the music world as Rolling Stone, Billboard, and SPIN to name just a few.

The searchable databases on AMG contain information about more than 200,000 individual albums, songs, and artists. A typical entry includes the AMG rating ranging from Best of Genre (a must-have album) to poor. Many of the entries for albums include a complete list of album tracks, and a list of all the people who worked on the album.

Databases are divided into top albums this week, popular, classical, music biographies, and music resources/information. This last database includes articles about musical styles, lists of mail-order catalogues, and music magazines. You can interact with the All Music Guide personnel through the message board. The folks who run the AMG encourage you to get in touch, tell them what's missing, and even add reviews and opinions of your own.

All Music Guide Forum (AMGPOP)

The All Music Guide Forum is the place to go to discuss what you've discovered in the AMG, or any other subject relevant to music. It is home to hundreds of messages about music of all varieties, from classical to rap. The library files, however, were old when we stopped in. Many of the entries were 18 months old or more. Since music and computers change so fast, the libraries may be better for people who want to explore the history of their favorite artists.

Rocknet Forum (ROCKNET) (T)

No doubt, in this forum you will find just about any kind of information or discussion about any kind of rock and roll you can think of. Whether or not you want your kids to visit is going to be up to you. Unlike some other places on CompuServe (such as the YDrive), Rocknet wasn't designed for kids. That's not to say they shouldn't go there, its just that the purpose of the forum is not for kids to enjoy rock and roll. The folks they meet here will be of all ages.

YDrive Forum (YDRIVE)

You'll find a complete discussion of the YDrive in

Chapter 6, TV and Movies. We include it here too, because its message boards and libraries include lots of discussion and information about music. The YDrive, designed expressly for kids, is a great place to let your kids go and explore.

Recording Industry Forum (RECORDING) (T)

This forum is for people who work in the music industry. The focus is far more business than entertainment, so your kids won't find much fun here. If you have a very serious musician, he'll probably enjoy the contact with people from many of the leading record companies, including RCA, Warner Bros., and Geffen Records.

Oldies Diner Forum (OLDIES)

This forum is dedicated to the music of America from 1955 to 1970. We're really stretching back here, but our kids would recognize a lot of this music simply because their parents are relics. If you regularly play music from the Forrest Gump years, your kids will recognize some of what's going on, too. To be honest, you'll probably head into this forum before they will, but who knows, they may someday need an old lyric from the days of hippies and bell-bottoms, and if they do, send them here.

Warner Bros. Song Preview (WBPREVIEW)

Come here to download 30-second .WAV sound files from many popular groups and performers on the Warner Bros. label. Keep in mind the size of the .WAV files. For example, a single file can take nearly 15 minutes to download, so they are not inexpensive to retrieve, and they take up considerable amounts of storage space once you've gotten them. Still, they are fun, and if one of your child's favorite performer happens to be listed, why not give her a treat once in a while?

PRODIGY

Music 1 BB (MUSIC) (+) (T)

Here is the meeting place on Prodigy for fans of Rock and Roll and Alternative music. The bulletin board staff is experienced in the world of music and music journalism. Lisa Robinson is the Board Leader. She is the rock columnist of the New York Post. She's traveled with bands including Led Zeppelin, The Rolling Stones, The Who, and Van Halen. She is also a member of the nominating committee for the Rock & Roll Hall of Fame.

With these credentials, you'd think this would be a great place for kids who love Rock music, but we were disappointed. The message boards were filled with chatter about sex, drugs, and violence. It probably is only a small group of people posting messages like that, but we can't encourage you to take your kids here. Someone at Prodigy should be doing some housecleaning on this board.

Music 2 BB (MUSIC) (+)

This is the place for people interested in all the other types of music besides Rock and Alternative. You won't find the same message content here, but you probably won't find your kids here either! The focus is on Classical, Jazz, Country & Western, New Age, Religious, and Big Band music.

Music Charts (MUSIC)

Come here to get the latest information on what's hot in categories that include Modern Rock, Rap, R&B, Country, Jazz, Classical, Pop, and Adult Contemporary. You'll also find information about the latest top-grossing concerts.

Guest Spotlight (GUEST SPOTLIGHT) (FREE)

Guest Spotlight is a menu that provides information about famous people who are scheduled to appear on Prodigy. Your time spent on the menu is free, so don't hesitate to let your kids stop by and see who's coming online.

From the Guest Spotlight, you can find out about appearances by famous people from the world of music, entertainment, and politics. These folks either make themselves available for answering BB message postings, or they appear in real-time chat sessions with Prodigy users. Prodigy maintains a BB Guest Archive so that you can see what previous guests had to say, including Mick Jagger and Tom Petty.

THE INTERNET

The World Wide Web
Music is one of the hottest topics on the Net. A check of Yahoo found more than 2800 music-related Web sites.

The Ultimate Band List
(http://american.recordings.com/wwwofmusic/ubl.html)
Here's the place to start exploring the Web's music resources. It's billed as the Web's largest interactive list of music links, and we don't doubt it. There are links not only to other music-related Web sites, but listings for newsgroups, mailing lists, FAQ files, and lyrics—all categorized by group or musician. Visitors can also add their own recommended links. The Internet at its best.

Virtual Radio
(http://www.microserve.net/vradio/)
Virtual Radio gives you the chance to download complete songs from what, to us, look to be obscure bands. The site is easy to use; the bands are listed on the Home Page for easy access (see Figure 7.5). Virtual Radio covers a wide range of music, from country to punk to heavy metal polka. There's music from around the world here and in a variety of languages, like the Blue Hearts in Japanese, from Japan.

Figure 7.5 Virtual Radio

At today's modem speeds, we don't think it's practical to routinely download music (450k to 900+k files are common). But there's a lot of other information here that young fans will like (in the News and Views area, for example).

The Digital Tradition Folk Song Database
(http://pubweb.parc.xerox.com/digitrad/titles/short)

This site offers a searchable database containing the words and music to thousands of folk songs. You can search by name or "keyword." Feeling middle aged one day, we searched under "aging" and came across "Those Were the Days" and the associated lyrics.

The Official Rolling Stones Web Site
(http://www.stones.com/) (T)

This is one of the best sites of its type (see Figure 7.6). Interviews, photos, music video—it's all here. Warning—the Rolling Stones Fiction Corner, where fans can post "Stones-based fiction," includes some

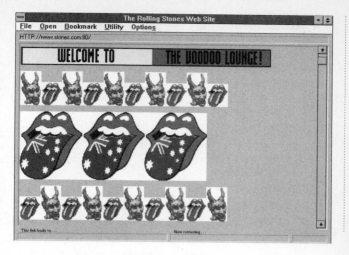

Figure 7.6 Rolling Stones WWW Home Page

language we wouldn't want our parents to see, let alone our 10-year old.

The Drums and Percussion Page
(http://www.cse.ogi.edu/Drum/)
There are many places on the net for your young musician to learn more about musical instruments. This site, for example, includes an encyclopedia of percussion instruments and how-to articles on topics such as drum tuning. The Webmaster envisions adding a section on warm-ups and exercises. "Ideally, you'd be able to hear a particular exercise and play along or over it."

Worldwide Internet Live Music Archive (WILMA)
(http://www.ddv.com/Wilma/)
Young concert-goers can turn here for live music details, including club and venue listings, an artist tour directory, and a concert and club reviews section (see Figure 7.7).

Figure 7.7 Worldwide Internet Live Music Archive (WILMA) Home Page

Newsgroups

There are over 70 newsgroups for music fans. Most have the prefix alt.fan or alt.music. We found newsgroups for Aerosmith, Beastie Boys, Bob Dylan, the Grateful Dead, Prince, Paul Simon, and a lot of groups we never heard of (but your kids probably know).

Like many other newsgroups, these have their share of snide comments, obscenities, flamers, etc. Of course, the newsgroup may reflect the personality of the subject and, in turn, that may have a bearing on who's posting messages there. The newsgroup devoted to "Christian gospel/pop music singer" Amy Grant had a decidedly different tone to it than the one devoted to The Beastie Boys Rap Group (no surprise there).

The safe thing to do, of course, would be to declare all of them off limits. And you can probably successfully do that in the case of 8- to 12-year-olds. But we think you're going to have some trouble keeping teens away from these groups once they find out about them. While compared to the blatantly sexually oriented newsgroups, they are tame, but brutal language does shows up.

What you'll find on music-related newsgroups:

○ Opinions about new releases
○ Media coverage of the celebrity
○ Concert tour information
○ Chat about their videos
○ Mentions of related net resources (e.g., Web sites)

THE BEST OF THE REST

eWorld

Music Universe (MU/MUSIC UNIVERSE) (T)
This one-stop music central includes artists' tour plans, interviews, as well as industry gossip and visual and sound files. Monitor your child's use of the associated bulletin board; we found some crude postings there.

8

Hobbies

The online world offers a wealth of information and experience for hobbyists of all ages. Never before have people had such an easy way to share their hobbies with other people from throughout the world. You will find online hobbyists have several common characteristics. They are serious about their hobbies. They are friendly and generous with their time and experience. They are happy to work with newcomers to both the hobby in question and the online world. You won't find a nicer group of people anywhere.

Every hobby you can think of is represented online. We're not exaggerating. If you can collect it, or make it, or research it, you can find people in cyberspace who are doing just that. It would be tedious and pointless for us to describe every online site there is for pursuing your hobbies. Instead, we thought we'd tell you about how some hobbyists use online services to pursue their hobbies in creative ways.

AMERICA ONLINE

Kids Only: Hobbies & Clubs (HOBBIES)
The first stop for any young hobbyist on America

Figure 8.1 Downloaded via Internet from wuarchive.wustl.edu

Online is the Kids Only menu. Here you will find a hot button devoted to hobbies and clubs (see Figure 8.2). Several Kids Only clubs were under construction when we visited the area. These were the Astronomy Club, the Environmental Club, and the Star Trek Club. If any of these appeal to your child, stop by and see what progress has been made in the last few months.

Figure 8.2 Kids Only Screen on America Online notice the Hobbies & Clubs hot button

Perhaps more important than those clubs that are already available in the Kids Only section, is the promise of the Kids Only staff to bring more clubs online in this area as the demand increases. If your child has a real passion for a particular hobby, why not drop the Kids Online staff members a note and see what you can do about getting an online club started.

The Kids Only section includes a message board devoted to hobbies and clubs. Here your child can read and leave messages from and for kids who share his hobbies. Some of the representative hobbies listed on the message board include: music, horses, magic, video games, Legos, kites, and the American Girls collector dolls. The message board had 46 of a possible 50 topic folders going when we were there, so as you can see, kids on America Online love to talk about their hobbies!

COMPUSERVE

CompuServe has forums for hobbyists and collectors of every variety. Your kids can stop in to chat and exchange information about their favorite hobbies, but they can also swap, trade, and buy items to complete their collections.

Handcrafts Forum (HANDCRAFT)

This is the home for anyone who loves to do all types of crafts, excluding fibercrafts. CompuServe has a separate forum for folks who like to work with fibers. Early in 1995, CompuServe's Crafts Forum split into two forums; Fibercrafts and Handcrafts. The old forum was so popular that the forum administrators had trouble keeping up with the traffic. Now messages stay posted on the message boards longer and conferences are easier to manage.

We chose to highlight this forum not only because the staff is so helpful and the members so friendly, but also because the library files are filled with dozens of craft ideas and instructions. If your kids love crafts, they can stop by these libraries and learn how to make just about anything. They'll find directions for the old standards such as pine cone turkeys and tissue paper flowers, but they can also learn how to make homemade plastiline and weave their own baskets.

Scott
CompuServe, 74132,274
Age: 14
Home: Philadelphia, PA, USA

We met Scott on the YDrive on CompuServe (see Chapter 6), and that's where you can find him too. He hangs out here to talk with friends and swap email messages. He is also an avid collector of sports cards and memorabilia. He believes being online has made a big difference in the way he pursues his hobbies. When we first spoke, Scott was celebrating his one-year anniversary online. We thought he sounded like an old pro. What do you think?

I have, through CompuServe, picked up some of my favorite players' addresses or favorite items. I bought a picture signed by Cosmo g Kramer for $15. I loved the movie "Grumpy Old Men" so I bought an old "Odd Couple" photo signed by Jack Lemmon and Walter Matthau. Autographs give me a chance to write and something to look forward to 300 days a year.

Now to the trading card front. I have traded with people everywhere, 30 some states, 4 Canadian provinces, Germany, and France. I have met people from everywhere, from Barrow, Alaska, to Jakarta, Indonesia. I did a deal with somebody in Nantes, France and in Stuttgart, Germany.

I completed a 50 card autographed baseball card set from Signature Rookies. It took more than 8 months to complete. I acquired 15 cards from trades with people on CompuServe, another 10 were purchased from people here online (including the last 2 I needed). With only 8650 of each card, signed sets are hard to come by. As a matter of fact, I know of 2 other people online who own complete sets.

PRODIGY

Make It (MAKE IT)

Your kids can stop in here to find directions for a fun craft they can make themselves (see Figure 8.3). Seven different categories of craft ideas include gifts, games, holiday projects, paper crafts, party ideas, outdoor projects, and crafts for younger kids. Your kids can find directions for making mosaic checkers, bird feeders, kites, pop-up cards, paper lanterns, and endless other crafts.

Figure 8.3 Prodigy's Make-It Screen

Kidnet

Hobbies

HOBBY AREAS ON THE MAJOR COMMERCIAL SERVICES

AMERICA ONLINE

Astronomy Forum
Cooking Forum
DC Comics Online
The Exchange
Genealogy Forum
HAM Radio Forum
Kodak Photo Forum
Popular Photog-
    raphy
Quilting Forum
Science Fiction &
    Fantasy Forum
Star Trek Forum
Trading Card Forum
The Trivia Forum
The Writer's Forum

COMPUSERVE

Astronomy
    Forum
Collectibles
    Forum
Cooking Forum
Fibercrafts Forum
Genealogy Forum
Hamnet Forum
Literary Forum
Model Aviation
    Forum
Photography
    Forum
Science Fiction &
    Fantasy
Trading Card
    Forum
TrainNet Forum

PRODIGY

Collecting BB
Crafts BB
Genealogy BB
Hobbies BB
Homelife BB
Trading Cards
    BB

THE INTERNET

The World Wide Web

The Internet offers an abundance of resources about every hobby imaginable. Whether your kids want more information about a current hobby, or want to try a new one, the Internet is an excellent place to turn.

A search of Yahoo found 130 Web sites under the category of Hobbies and Crafts. There's everything from Amateur Radio to Woodworking. The table on the next page gives you just a sample. It's possible to find more than one site devoted to a hobby. Postcard collecting has several for example, including some from collectors. Amateur Radio held the record with a full 88 resources mentioning it. Most of the others had at least several.

SAMPLES OF WEB SITES FOR HOBBIES

Amateur radio
Antiques
Balloon Modeling
Birding
Collectors
Companies
Crochet
Embroidery
Flowers
Gardening
Juggling
Kites

Knitting
Magic
Models
Origami
Photography
Prospecting
Rockets
Rocks, Gems, and Minerals
String Figures
Textiles
Woodworking

Isaac
The Internet
Age: 14
Home: Los Angeles, CA
Kids who use the Internet may develop new hobbies as a result of their time online. Here's the story of one who made his new hobby pay off!

I'm an HTML consultant. What that means is that I help people design World Wide Web pages using HTML, the HyperText Markup Language. I learned this language in the summer of 1994 when I was talking to one of my friends in email and he told me how cool it was. I downloaded a help file from NCSA (National Center for Supercomputing Applications), I read it, and began putting up pages. Now that I've become rather proficient at programming and designing Web pages, I've started to get paid for it.

Currently, I'm working on helping a company put up a webserver with which to create a "mall" to sell their products. To me, the Web is a constantly evolving organism. It's always changing, and as long as you have access to a few megabytes of space on a webserver, anyone can put up their own pages.

The Model Horse Web Page
(http://fohnix.metronet.com/HomePage/kira/model-horse/mhnew.html)

This site featured a lot of information about the origins of this hobby, which involves creating, collecting, and showing equine miniatures (see Figure

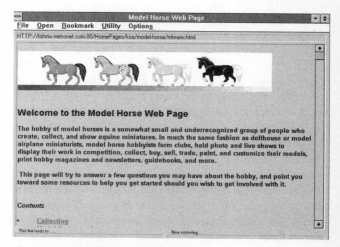

Figure 8.4 Model Horse WWW Home Page

8.4). There's information here for someone who is new to the hobby, as well as references and resources for old hands. Future plans call for listings of live "shows" where hobbyists display their horses in different classes and compete for ribbons (as in a real horse show). Webmaster Jackie Hamilton tells us that the hobby includes a lot of 8 to 14 year olds.

Stamp Collectors
(http://www.mbnet.mb.ca/~-lampi/stamps.html)
If your child is into the "wonderful little shapes that travel the world and make many people happy," she'll find other collectors to link up with here. The Webmaster, Jill Lampi, includes a link to her own home page. Through her page, kids can browse a list of people seeking keypals.

The Wooden Toy
(http://www.pd.astro.it/forms/mostra/mostra_i.html)
An electronic exhibit featuring descriptions and images of old wooden toys, in several categories. Neat! Most are from Italy, which is where this site originates.

Lego Information
(http://legowww.homepages.com/)
Okay, there's some promotional information about the Lego product line, including a parts list here, but your kids will also find some really cool things at this site (see Figure 8.5). There are lots of Lego ideas and activities, including games and computer-related Lego fun. Skip the tour of the Lego plant—it's one long text file.

U.S. Scouting Front Door
(http://iquest.com/~-hyper/Scouts/)
Turn here for information on badge requirements, scouting FAQs, and details on scouting activities and events (see Figure 8.6). There are separate pages for Cub Scouts, Boy Scouts/Varsity Scouts, Explorers, Order of the Arrow, Girl Scouts, and International Scouting.

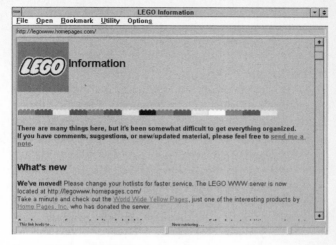

Figure 8.5 Lego WWW Home Page

KFS: Kite Fliers Site
(http://twoshakes.kfs.org/kites/)

This site shows the potential of the Web to pull together related information from places all over the

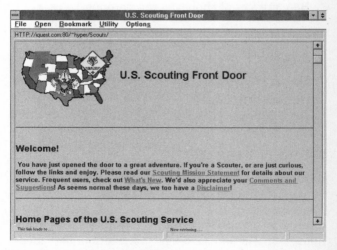

Figure 8.6 Scouting WWW Home Page

155

Net. For example, it includes links from the rec.kites archive on building kites; galleries of pictures from kiting enthusiasts; and assorted plans for kites.

Newsgroups

The Internet's hobbyist newsgroups have many equivalents among the forums and special interest groups on commercial online services. As usual, it's a tradeoff. The commercial services offer better organization and administration. The Internet newsgroups are, by and large, less expensive to use but untamed.

There's plenty of useful information to be found, but sometimes it comes with an "attitude." If you're coming across as mercenary you might get flamed. But, considering everything, the newsgroups are an excellent place to go for advice. These people are serious about their hobbies!

A fair question is whether or not young kids use these newsgroups much, especially those new to a particular hobby. Judging from the postings we read, it wouldn't appear so. So if your kids are really new to a hobby, they would be better off using a forum from one of the commercial online services.

Here are sample hobbyist newsgroups:

    rec.collecting.stamps
    rec.railroad
    rec.photo.help
    rec.woodworking
    rec.roller-coaster
    rec.scouting

THE BEST OF THE REST

GEnie
Stamp Collecting RoundTable (STAMPS)
The purpose of the Stamp Collecting RoundTable is to provide a forum for stamp collectors, dealers, and hobby writers to exchange information and ideas. Non-commercial trading of stamps is permitted.

9

Sports

Your young athletes can travel through cyberspace to a galaxy of virtual sports events. Your kids can go online to check the headlines or stats about their favorite teams, discuss plays and players, or join in a fantasy league and play the game. Sports online is more than a collection of games, it's a way of life for people who just can't get enough!

AMERICA ONLINE

Sports is such a vital activity on America Online that the service's main menu includes a hot button to take your kids directly to the sports features. This hot button takes them to a sports screen of other hot buttons where they'll find the features described below. Because America Online uses hot buttons for these features, some of our descriptions don't include keywords. Of course, because the online world changes so quickly, you'll want to check this menu for yourself to see what's new since we wrote this book.

The Grandstand (GRANDSTAND)
The Grandstand is a central gathering place for sports

Figure 9.1 Downloaded via Internet from wuarchive.wustl.edu

fans of every variety (see Figure 9.2). In addition to the latest news from all corners of the sports world, you will find message boards galore. Message boards abound for every sport from college football to professional hockey to martial arts, to sports car racing or collecting sports cards.

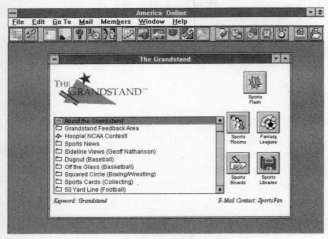

Figure 9.2 The Grandstand on America Online

The Grandstand is also the home for fantasy teams and simulated play. Fantasy play allows you to take part in a fantasy team of your own creation. Managers vie for the players they want on their teams. When the teams are formed, the leagues operate based on the statistics generated by the real players. Simulation play allows you to actually simulate a game, whether that be basketball or auto racing. Both fantasy games and simulations often require a fee to participate.

Jerry Pectol, Director of Online Activities for the Grandstand, explained more about how this works. If your child wants to play simulated football, for example, you must first buy the software for the game, such as Front Page Sports Football 95. Your child uses the software to refine his team and work the players in practice sessions. Then he turns in his coaching sheets to show the League Leader how his team works. The Leader creates a schedule showing your child who he will play each week.

Next, your child has to prepare his team for the competitions. If, for example, his opponent has Emmit Smith on her team, he better prepare his defense. Playing the game not only means taking care of your own team, but also scouting your competition and learning your opponent's tendencies.

The leagues are serious and time-consuming hobbies. Many of your child's opponents will be grown-ups. Jerry began charging fees to play when he saw that some people were signing up and creating teams, but not sticking with the play throughout the whole season. This left the schedule full of holes with no one to replace those teams and managers who quit. So, deciding to play a simulated game is a real commitment of time and energy.

Jerry says that simulated wrestling is especially popular with kids. In this sport, each player takes on the persona of a famous wrestler. Wrestlers meet online for live action matches. Each player inputs a move. The Referee commands the system to roll the dice and determine who gets the move. Then he works to make the outcome as realistic as possible. These matches include plenty of play-acting and wrestling type posturing.

You can even hop onto the message board in your wrestling persona and leave messages that you think would come straight from your wrestler. Jerry warns that this is where kids sometimes cross the line between fantasy and reality. If your kids decide to give it a try, remind them to address and insult the wrestler, not the player behind the wrestler. If the insults get out of hand, Jerry or one of his staff members will step in and gently remind the players that this is, after all, a game.

You can feel good about your kids exploring sports online at the Grandstand. People who have lots of experience with both cyberspace and kids are working there. They do their best to assure a secure environment where sports fans can explore and play. The games, although they often cost money, are stimulating and complicated. Your kids can certainly stretch their math, creative thinking, and problem solving skills while they trade players, strategize plays, and head into competition with other teams.

Sports News (SPORTS NEWS)
A click on this icon takes you to the latest news in the world of sports. If a story is breaking fast, your child can hop right here to get the latest scoop long before tomorrow's sports page hits the streets. You can also search the files of yesterday's news to track a story that has already happened.

Iditarod Trail Sled Dog Race (IDITAROD)
When we were researching this book, the Iditarod race had just begun in Anchorage, Alaska. The race covers about 1,150 miles between Anchorage and Nome, and lasts approximately 11 or 12 days. Through America Online, you could check in for a daily news update about the race (see Figure 9.3). Biographies, complete with photos, of the mushers helped put human faces on the racers' names.

Mitch Seavey, one of the mushers, submitted a daily diary. Mitch described his work leading up to the time of the race. These diary entries were filled with fascinating facts (did you know beaver meat is the best food for sled dogs?), and tremendous spirit as this musher prepared to meet his great challenge. He shared his concerns and goals with the readers. He was less concerned with winning the race than he was with racing well. His goal, leading up to the race, was to come away satisfied that his effort was the best he could make it.

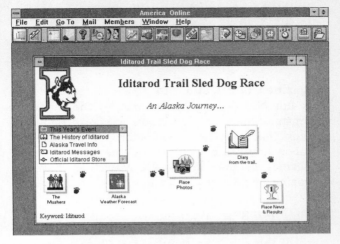

Figure 9.3 The Iditarod Trail Sled Dog Race on America Online

The message boards were filled with messages from students and teachers who were using the Iditarod as a jumping off point for schoolwork and discussions. An Official Iditarod Store rounds out the offerings with a place to buy every Iditarod thing from caps to sweats to stuffed husky pups.

When you visit, this Iditarod hot button will have been replaced with another more topical sports event. For example, March Madness followed the Iditarod. This hot button is reserved for detailed coverage of major sports events as they take place, each lasting several weeks to a month.

ABC Sports (ABC SPORTS)

This is the online home for the powerful ABC Sports machine. Here your child can read the latest news, view pictures and clips from sports events, write to ABC Sports, participate in message boards with the people at ABC Sports, and buy logoed apparel or sports videos. She can also play sports trivia games and participate in sports polls. The trivia games are not terribly rewarding. When you respond to the

161

question, you don't get any feedback about whether or not your answers are correct. Rather, your responses get compiled with everyone elses' and the results of the trivia quiz are posted weekly.

Magazines, Clubs, and Info

This hot button takes your child to the menu of forums and magazines dedicated to sports. He'll find forums that include the Aviation forum, BikeNet, Outdoor Adventure Online, and the Scuba Forum. Magazines include Backpacker Magazine, Bicycling Magazine, and Boating Magazine.

Local Coverage

This hot button brings to your screen the online versions of the sports sections of the Chicago Tribune, the New York Times, the San Jose Mercury, and Data-Times Sports. DataTimes is an online service featuring the full text from scores of newspapers. Services included in these sections range from straight headline news to commentary to message sections where you can talk to still more sports fans!

COMPUSERVE

Sports Forum (FANS)

Your kids can stop here on CompuServe for fantasy games including fantasy baseball, football, and hockey. They can also enter College/Pro football contests and Super Bowl contests. There are no fees for entering fantasy play in the Sports Forum.

The fantasy sports teams are incredibly popular online. Let's use a baseball fantasy as an example. In the Sports Forum, your child can choose to lead either an American League team or a National League team. Team rosters include 23 players and there are 12 teams in each league. The statistics for these players are tracked throughout the season, and prizes are awarded at the end of the season for the fantasy team with the most points.

Sports Illustrated Online (SPORTS)

Every Wednesday, the text and several photos from this weekly magazine are available on CompuServe (see Figure 9.4). Online users also get the opportunity to interact with the writers, editors, and other readers of Sports Illustrated through the Sports Illustrated Forum (SIFORUM).

Maybe the most complicated thing about using the Sports Illustrated Online area is the pricing structure that applies. Browsing through the magazine or using the SI Forum are charged at CompuServe's basic connect time rates, as is sending letters to the Sports Illustrated editors. Accessing the SI archives includes connect time rates plus a charge of $1.50 for each article. Time spent in the SI Store is free from connect charges.

The News, Scores, & Stats hot button brings you news from the Associated Press and the Sports Network. Your kids can check out the latest headlines and statistics here. They can also choose to take a look at news of a particular sport. For example, if they choose the Pro Football icon, they will move to

Figure 9.4 The Sports Illustrated Screen on CompuServe

another screen that again offers a variety of services as well as a list of relevant AP stories.

Still more Fantasy Sports games are also available through the Sports Illustrated Sports Services. Check out the main screen (SPORTS) for fees and details if you wish to play fantasy sports.

Associated Press Online: Sports (APO)

If your child wants to check out the latest sports headlines, show her how to get to AP Sports from the AP Online menu. AP Online is part of CompuServe's basic service offering. When she enters the go word APO, she'll go to the AP Online menu. From here she can choose Sports. Now she can read the latest news about baseball, football, basketball, hockey, soccer, college sports, tennis/golf, and Olympic or other sports. She can also check out the scoreboards for current sports events. This feature is a part of CompuServe's basic service offerings.

If she enters APSPORTS as her go command, she will enter a surcharged area of AP News Service that costs $15 per hour to use. Although she may find stories of slightly more depth under APSPORTS, she can probably get all the news she needs at the basic rate. In the APSPORTS area, she can also use a sports news clipping service. She can arrange, for example, to have every late-breaking story about this year's World Series delivered to her automatically. This carries yet another additional charge. These services are expensive, and their costs mount quickly. We advise you to stick with the news available through the basic service offering of AP Online.

Archive Photo Forum (ARCHIVE)

We could have featured this forum in several chapters in this book, but once we saw the images of Hank Aaron, Mickey Mantle, and Joe Louis, we thought it belonged here with sports. The photos available in this forum are the property of Archive

Photos, a leading source of historical engravings, drawings, and photos. We'd like to have shown you one, but the copyright laws expressly forbid the photos to be used for anything but personal pleasure.

A trip through the library files will turn up images of the world's most famous athletes. Complete directions are available for downloading and viewing the images. If you can't find the sports hero you're looking for, leave a message on the board. Someone is sure to know where you can find it, or forum staff will add it to the library if that is possible. Archive Photos owns more than 20,000,000 photos, so chances are good they'll have what you need.

NCAA Collegiate Sports Network (NCAA)
This is the online spot for information about the world of college sports. Your sports enthusiast will find all the stats necessary to stay happily informed about college basketball, football, baseball, softball, and volleyball. There is also information about schedules, championship playoffs, and news releases (although when we stopped in, the latest news was three months old). Still, during certain times of the year, such as the NCAA's Final Four countdown, beginning in March, you'll find lots of up-to-date information here.

Other Forums
If your child has an interest, CompuServe probably has a forum for other people who do too. Here is a list of some sports-related forums your child might want to explore.

- America's Cup Forum
- Motor Sports Forum
- Outdoor Activities Forum
- Outdoors Library
- Sailing Forum

- Sports Simulation Forum
- Tennis Forum
- The Great Outdoors Forum
- Trading Card Forum

PRODIGY

Sports Illustrated for Kids

Your kids can find a version of Sports Illustrated for Kids under the New for Kids hot button on the Kids screen. They can stop in here to read articles, leave messages for the editors, or check out what's hot this month in sports. Ask the Athlete puts your kids directly in touch with a featured athlete. When we were there, Andre Agassi was taking questions from kids.

The SI for Kids bulletin board is a plus feature, but your kids can stop here to discuss whatever's on their sports minds.

The Sports Illustrated for Kids Challenge (SIFK Challenge) is a trivia game set on a colorful football field. Players advance up the field by answering questions about all types of sports, from the Olympics to basketball to figure skating. This game is a core service offering, and it's fun and easy to play.

The NFL Online Fanclub (NFL FAN)

During the football season, this is the place to talk football. Your kids can come here to check the scoreboard, read the latest news, buy NFL merchandise, or jump to the NFL bulletin board (a plus feature). In the off season, when we were here, the welcome screen was free of connect time charges, and at the core rate, news stories of off-season happenings were still being posted.

Prodigy's Sports Screen (SPORTS)

From Prodigy's Main Menu, your kids will find a Sports/ESPNET hot button. This takes them to the main menu for sports offerings on Prodigy (see Figure

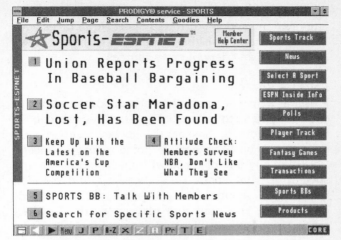

Figure 9.5 Prodigy's Sports Screen

9.5). Today's most current headlines are here, along with a list of other hot buttons that will lead to specific sports information and features.

Sports Track
This is Prodigy's version of your kids' own sports news clipping service for scores and schedules from their favorite teams. They can choose up to 24 teams to track; from major league baseball, football, basketball, and hockey. They can also track college football or basketball, depending on the season. After they personalize their Sports Track, they will automatically receive relevant new information. They will have the latest scoop on their favorite teams at the touch of a button.

News
This hot button calls up a menu of sports/news options that include AP Online Sports, International Sports News, Quick Sports, and Sports News. AP Online Sports gives your kids the latest sports news coming across the AP wire. International Sports highlights sports news such as world figure skating and

track competitions. Quick Sports presents a single late breaking sports story, and Sport News takes your kids to a menu showing a handful of recent news stories from a variety of news sources.

Select A Sport
Pressing Select A Sport shows your kids a menu of choices specific to individual sports. They can choose baseball, football, basketball, hockey, tennis, golf, auto racing, bowling, boxing, horse racing, or soccer. Choosing any one of these will take them to an area specific to that sport. Here they will find detailed information about the leagues, competitions, schedules, teams, statistics, and players for the featured sport. This is almost like having a separate news service for each sport your kids follow.

ESPN Inside Information
This is the online home of the cable network ESPN. Kids can come here to find biographies for all their favorite ESPN personalities. They'll also find the latest news in sports from ESPN, and a Chris Berman sound clip welcomes them to the page. Everything that is specific to ESPN and its coverage of the world of sports is happening online here.

Polls
Prodigy loves user polls and here kids can stop by to voice their opinions about the latest sports happening or read the results of recent polls.

Player Track (Plus)
Player Track does for your kids' favorite players what Sports Track does for their favorite sports. It is meant to be used in conjunction with Prodigy's fantasy baseball game play. Kids can keep track automatically of the statistics they'll need to follow their fantasy teams. They may have as many as 50 entries on their track. Tracks are available for both football and baseball players.

Transactions

Click on this hot button and your kids will find the latest news on the most recent transactions in sports. Whether the headline is the trade of their favorite baseball star or the sale of their favorite football team, if its transacting, they'll find news of it here.

Sports BBs (Plus)

In addition to the bulletin boards already mentioned, this hot button calls up a list of sports-related bulletin boards.

Sports BB (SPORTS BB) (Plus)

This is the place on Prodigy to play fantasy sports games. As on all of the services already discussed, these games are lively and popular.

Sports Play BB (SPORTS PLAY BB) (Plus)

This is the bulletin board for people who want to talk about their own sports activity. Your kids will find messages here from people of all ages who play every sport you can imagine. They can stop in here for some tips on batting or punting, or to share their latest soccer victory.

THE INTERNET

The World Wide Web

There are more than 1,300 Web sites devoted to sports. Over 80 of them cover soccer alone!

Kids love to follow professional sports teams. What a treat to be able to get the inside scoop, complete with pictures! By the time you read this, there's a good chance your child's favorite team will have a place on the Internet. Use Yahoo or another search engine to track it down.

At the time of this writing, ESPN had plans to deliver "the most advanced online sports information service to fans around the world." Again, use Yahoo or WebCrawler to search for it.

World Wide Web of Sports Site
(http://www.tns.lcs.mit.edu/cgi-bin/sports).

Your young sports fan should start his Web explorations here. It's got it all: NBA basketball highlights, including video from last night's games; NCAA basketball stats, including the major polls; and similar information for football, sailing, baseball, hockey, auto racing, cycling, volleyball, soccer, even frisbees. There's even preliminary information about the upcoming 1998 Olympic games in Nagano. There's also a link to Sports Illustrated's new Web Site, which you can reach directly at (http://www.pathfinder. com/si/greet.html)

The WWW Sports Information Service
(http://www.netgen.com/sis/sports.html)

Another good launching pad, this was the winner of the Best Entertainment Site in the Best of Web '94 contest. A page of top-notch links, its creators say that from here you can get "every little bit of data about your favorite professional sport ." Could be.

WWW Virtual Library of Sports
(http://www.atm.ch.cam.ac.uk/sports/sports.html)

International sports links galore! Where else can you find links to a hare and hounds home page, one on biking in West Virginia, and another about rowing in Stockholm? This is sure to broaden your sports fan's outlook on the world.

The US Soccer Web Page
(http://www.cs.cmu.edu:8001/afs/cs/usr/mdwheel/w ww/soccer/us-soccer.html)

Kids love soccer, so they should also love this "page for soccer fans by soccer fans" (see Figure 9.6). There's lots here, including information about the U.S. national team, U.S. pro leagues, information for soccer fans worldwide such as magazines, and mailing lists; and links to other soccer pages.

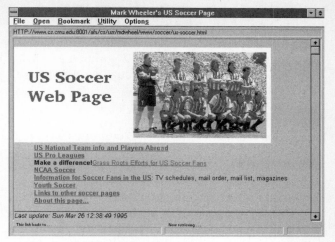

Figure 9.6 Soccer WWW Home Page

A separate Youth Soccer page was under construction when we visited, but it had the makings of a good site. Plans were for it to include details on youth soccer organizations and tournament announcements.

The NBA Web Site
(http://www.nando.net/sports/bkb/1194/nba/nba.html) (T)
This has features under the heading NBA Today, and game scores by Conference. The writing is aimed at adults, although older kids will be able to get something from this. Fantasy League basketball, which enables you to run your own league, is part of this site.
The Basketball server (from the same people who bring you the baseball server) is equally comprehensive.

The World Wide Web Tennis Server
(http://arganet.tenagra.com/Racquet–Workshop/Tennis.html)

Your budding Wimbledon pros should come here for their tennis news and details on equipment. What a wealth of information! Aside from the stats from recent matches, there's plenty of equipment advice and some tips from players (although we'd like to see more of those).

Fantasy Baseball
(http://www.cm.cf.ac.uk/User/Gwyn.Price/fantasy_baseball/)

Players pretend they're managing their own teams, with real major league players. You aim for the World Series by managing better than other fantasy league managers. If it all sounds fanciful, it is; but players really get into it. This page is a complete resource to fantasy baseball, with many links to newsgroups, archives, and other web sites of interest. Fantasy baseball is "very popular with kids," according to Gwyn Price, Webmaster for this page. While most players are older, "this is changing, and the guy who won the league I played in last year was 13!" said Gwyn.

The Global Cycling Network
(http://www.cycling.org/)

This site links cyclists from all over the world. Young cyclists can really feel connected to other cyclists, whether they're next door or on another continent. Look for details on cycling organizations, mailing lists, books, and meetings relevant to bicycling.

The Figure Skating Home Page
(http://www.cs.yale.edu/HTML/YALE/CS/HyPlans/loosemore-sandra/skate.html)

Skate on over to see FAQs on competitive figure skating, pictures of skaters, and even a technical figure skating page featuring movies and pictures of jumps and spins. Sandra Loosemore, who runs this page, says it's actually intended for adults "but I think kids who are interested in skating wouldn't have any serious problem understanding the writing. I have no intention of including any of the various X-rated pictures of Tonya Harding that have been circulating on the Net, either, if that's a concern."

Sandra not only has morals and a fondness for figure skating, she likes frogs. She maintains the net's Froggy Page (http://www.cs.yale.edu/HTML/YALE/CS/HyPlans/loosemore-sandra/froggy.html). She's combined her two interests by creating pictures of "frogs on ice." For an example see Chapter 13. These pictures proved so popular she created a second frogs on ice page.

The Great Outdoor Recreation Page (GORP)
(http://www.gorp.com/)

Hikers, bikers, climbers, birdwatchers, and skiers will find many links here to useful information (see Figure 9.7). By traveling along this site, kids can understand and appreciate the diversity of nature, wildlife, geography, and world cultures. GORP also describes many of our protected lands, including national parks, forests, national wildlife refuges, and even national monuments.

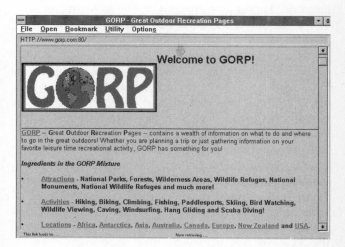

Figure 9.7 Welcome to GORP WWW Home Page

SPOTLIGHT ON JAKE WILLIAMS

Note: The following profile is a shortened version of a profile that appears in the Internet's Academy One WWW site. It's an example of the valuable and unique information kids can find on the Net. For more information about Academy One, see Chapter 5.

I became a professional heavyweight fighter in 1953. I fought professionally from 1953 through 1961. I was billed as "Jolting Jake Williams, the Boys' Town Bomber" in my first fight at Hollywood Legion Stadium. I was undefeated in my first ten bouts. In fact, I remained undefeated for two years.

Soon fighting became a way of life. My routine was fairly consistent. Every morning, the alarm clock went off at 4:00 A.M. My feet hit the floor immediately. I'd pull on my trunks, sweat suit, cap, and sneakers and off I'd dash to do my road work.

One of my best fights was my return main event bout with Irish Jimmy Sheets. The press considered this rematch "One of the year's thrillers." My father, some of my college buddies, and several celebrities were in attendance. Thus, in retrospect, I must have felt the need to "be colorful" during the fight, when I really should have had my eyes on my opponent. I recall briefly, smiling and acknowledging someone who was waving at the ringside during the fight. The next thing I remember was hearing someone far, far off in the distance counting 6–! Six, I thought, where am I? What's happening? As I began to come out of a foggy haze, I realized that the referee was counting, and that I was lying flat on my back in the ring. What ever happened to 1,2,3,4, and 5? By the time the referee had counted to seven, I was up on one knee. People have subsequently told me that my father was running all around the arena during this brief interlude in the bout shouting, "Stop the fight! Throw in the towel!" By the time the referee had counted to eight, I was up on both feet. During this fight, Jimmy knocked me down twice. I decked him three times. I went on to win the fight.

I won a few fights, and I lost a few. In 1960, I fought the number two contender, Alejandro Laverente, the Argentinean Champion. After that fight, I retired at the ripe old age of 29. This was, coincidentally, the year that Muhammed Ali became a professional fighter.

Upon my retirement from the professional fight game, I had an opportunity to reflect upon the very beginning of my boxing career. It was without a doubt motivated by Boy's Town's Boxing Coach, Paul Hartnick, a Creighton University graduate. Because of Coach Hartnick, I won the 1947 and 1948 all-state heavyweight boxing championships in Nebraska. Because of this dedicated coach, I was able to compete with the "best of them" on a professional basis.

Although I'd been involved in athletics as a youth, I never thought I'd become a professional fighter—not in my fondest dreams! Father Flanagan of Boys Town said, "leisure time programs are most essential in this day and age, when we have so much leisure time. Then, too, a hobby today may become a vocation tomorrow." Father Flanagan's predictions certainly became true in my case. Boxing had become my profession.

Note: The original source for this profile is Williams, Leona C. and Jarrod B.; Profiles in Restitution: Father Flanagan Boys Town. Riverside, CA 1987.

Newsgroups

Sports-related newsgroups are one of the few categories of newsgroups (outside of those clearly earmarked for kids) where we saw postings from kids. Here are some of the ways in which fans are using these newsgroups.

The skating newsgroup (rec.skate) is full of people who take skating VERY seriously, and are uniformly polite. There's no flaming here! One young fan was looking for other Nancy Kerrigan fans.

On rec.equestrian, there were postings from those seeking solace from fellow temporarily horseless emailers; On rec.sport, baseball fans were arguing about who was the greatest base stealer of all time, and over in rec.bicycles.misc, someone wanted a recommendation for a good bicycling magazine "for someone riding a mountain bike on trails for camping purposes." That one was answered by a few people: *BIKE* and *Dirt Rag* were cited. We guess that proves you can find an answer to anything on the Internet. The basketball newsgroup (rec.sport.basketball) was the raunchiest of those we checked out, and probably isn't a place for kids.

Eventually, we expect we'll see a lot more newsgroups for kids, and sports would be a likely area in which we'll see them.

THE BEST OF THE REST

Delphi

Young America

Young America is one of the 10 teams that competed for the America's Cup sailing trophy in 1995. During the running of the race your kids could stay in touch with the team members through Delphi. When the New Zealand team won, fans celebrated online! The full service may not be available by the time you read this book, but journal entries, activity logs, and messages may be retained after the race is over. You can also look for this site on the Internet. It's a Web site. Use the keywords Young America to find it.

10

Ecology
and the World

Most of the kids we know are deeply concerned about the environment and the ecological health of our planet. With online connections rapidly shrinking the distances between us, your kids can use their online time to learn about ecological problems and to work on solving them, too.

AMERICA ONLINE

Kids Only Environmental Club (KIDS)

When we were writing this book, the Environmental Club in the Kids Only section was under construction. Until that construction is complete, the area includes some files from other environmental areas of America Online. They are easy for kids to access and use under the Hobbies & Clubs hot button on the Kids Only menu.

Among these features are the Ecological Directory, the Network Earth Resource Library, and a listing of Environmental Organizations. We'll talk about these

Figure 10.1 Downloaded via Internet from wuarchive.wustl.edu

in more detail below. When the Environmental Club is complete (and it probably is by now), your kids will have a place to discuss and plan environmental projects with other kids.

Ecological Directory (KIDS)
This directory is produced by environmental journalist P.J. Grimes. It lists products and people and their environmental work. Your child can use this to find sources of products from the rain forest, recycled products, or organizations dedicated to preserving endangered species. It's an online warehouse of information about every type of product and organization dedicated to preserving and improving the world's environment.

Network Earth Online (NETWORK EARTH)
This online site was created in conjunction with Turner Broadcasting (TBS) to go along with its environmental magazine TV series, Network Earth (see Figure 10.2). The show and the service highlight important environmental issues in the news. They also profile people who are finding solutions to environmental problems and sharing those solutions with others who want to help.

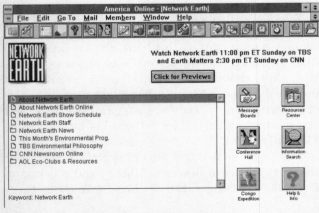

Figure 10.2 Network Earth on America Online

Network Earth Online allows you to communicate directly with the show's producers and other viewers. The message boards in this forum are divided into two areas. One is to discuss environmental issues, and one is an action center that proposes programs and activities to help the environment. In this latter section, we found several folders devoted to kids and their environmental work.

Forum members were proposing online clubs, letter-writing campaigns, and programs to appeal to world leaders on a variety of issues. This is the place if your kids are concerned about the environment and are eager to roll up their sleeves and get to work.

Environmental Organizations (KIDS)

Here you'll find a listing of hundreds of organizations, associations, and businesses interested in improving or protecting the environment. Your child is sure to find the organization that is working to promote her special environmental cause, whether that is the ethical treatment of animals, or the advancement of renewable energy sources.

Environmental Forum (EFORUM)

This is the meeting place for people devoted to ecology. It is also the original home of the Ecology Directory and the list of Ecological Organizations described above, so some of the valuable information generated in this forum is already available to your kids directly from the KIDS menu. The message boards in this forum are populated by adults. Your kids may not be all that interested in contributing to the discussions.

The Nature Conservancy (NATURE) (T)

The Nature Conservancy has been operating in the United States for 40 years. It preserves plants, animals, and natural communities by protecting the land and water they need to survive. The online home of the Nature Conservancy includes an online version of

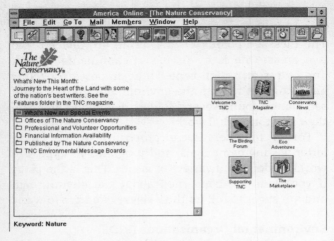

Figure 10.3 The Nature Conservancy on America Online

its magazine, a Birding Forum for birdwatchers, and live interviews with people prominent in the field of conservation (see Figure 10.3).

COMPUSERVE

Earth Forum (EARTH)

The Earth Forum on CompuServe is a serious place. Most of the members are adults, and many of the issues they discuss will be beyond all but the most mature kids. Aside from this, the Earth Forum is a very valuable source of information about animal rights and the preservation of endangered species, and the members accomplish a lot of work (see Figure 10.4). If you have a serious environmentalist, bring him here.

When we visited, there was a sample letter addressed to an executive of a large record company. It seems that, in the name of performance art, one of the bands signed to the record label had tortured and killed a chicken during a live performance. This letter was calling for the record executive to

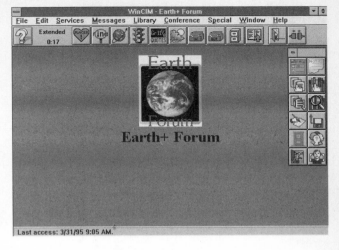

Figure 10.4 The Earth Forum on CompuServe

see to it that this behavior would not be repeated. It was ready to be saved, printed, and adapted by anyone interested in joining the campaign to prevent a repeat performance of this violence. There were also many other letters describing animals in need and ways that humans can start helping them. This is a place where your kids can come and take an active role in trying to help improve the world.

The forum libraries also contain files with lots of activities kids can do to explore the environment. Your kids can find directions for planting a butterfly garden, turning part of your yard into a meadow, and surveying your neighborhood for wildlife that lives right under their noses!

Outdoor News Clips (OUTNEWS) (+)
Here's a collection of the latest newswire stories relevant to the environment. If your child needs up-to-the-minute news about such a current event, check here.

PRODIGY

MayaQuest (MAYAQUEST)

MayaQuest cyclists took off on a twelve-week expedition that began in the winter of 1995. They rode bicycles exploring ancient Mayan ruins throughout Central America, including Guatemala, Mexico, Belize, and Honduras. During the expedition, kids used Prodigy to keep in touch with the cyclists (see Figure 10.5). Kids went online to meet the team, vote on their next destination, and learn about the Mayan Civilization. Throughout the expedition, kids could download maps and sites of the team's visits. They could also view images of both ancient Mayan artifacts and life as it exists today in the rain forest.

Several times each week, the team sent Prodigy trip updates. Kids could also interact with the team right from the MayaQuest menu. Pressing the hot button *Talk to the Team* took you to the Adventure Bulletin Board (Plus), the home of the MayaQuest message board. The board was a lively place where kids

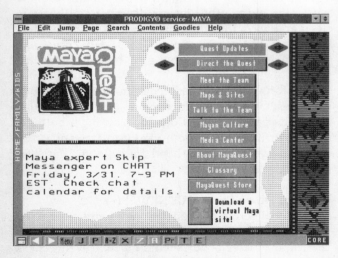

Figure 10.5 The MayaQuest Screen on Prodigy

could interact with the team members and each other. The team actually posted regular questions to the kids online to see what their opinions were, based on the knowledge they were gaining from observing the trip.

When the trip was over, Prodigy users enjoyed a wrap-up of the adventure. They also voted to see where the team would go next. The team began planning their next adventure within one week of returning from the MayaQuest.

Space Challenge (SPACE)

Check here to put your kids in touch with NASA as it prepares for the next launch of the Space Shuttle. When we visited, they were reliving the STS—66 Atmospheric Laboratory for Applications and Science Spacelab missions. (ATLAS-3).

For your space buffs, you'll find a question/answer interview between Prodigy and NASA. Scientific phenomenon such as G-Force, thrust, and physical laws of rocket science are explained and discussed. Read descriptions and explanations about how space suits work. And what about telepresence? We learned it means using a computer and a robot to extend the field of your senses to remote locations. That's a pretty amazing idea.

Highlighted words appear throughout the text. Clicking on the highlights gives you a quick explanation of terms you may not understand or ideas you want explained in more detail. The Space Calendar was the only disappointment. When we stopped in, during March, the calendar listings were for the previous October, November, and December; not too helpful for planning ahead. Still, there's plenty of fascinating stuff here for kids who are curious about space.

Ocean Challenge (OCEAN)

Prodigy hooked up with Rich Wilson and Bill Biewenga as they sailed from San Francisco around

ARRIVAL UPDATE

SAN FRANCISCO

BOSTON

OCEAN
CHALLENGE

Read Rich and
Bill's letters on
how it feels to be
back!

····· NORTHERN
LIGHT
····· GREAT
AMERICAN II

> INTRODUCTION

Menu J P A-Z X   Pr T E   CORE

Figure 10.6 The Ocean Challenge Screen on Prodigy

Cape Horn to Boston (see Figure 10.6). They were racing to beat a record for this trip that was in place for 140 years. The record of 76 days, 6 hours was set by the Northern Light clipper ship. The voyage began early in January 1995 and continued through the middle of March. Updates appeared at noon every Monday, Wednesday, and Friday.

Visitors could read the ship's log and exact map-position, and they could exchange questions and answers with the two sailors. The Ocean Challenge menu was updated every week with a new number. Clicking on that number (corresponding to the weeks of the voyage) took you to NOVA and National Geographic features describing that part of the world.

Throughout the trip, activities were planned and described for kids to do offline. Step-by-step directions taught kids how to make and use a sextant and a barometer. Other activities allowed them to test their understanding of the physical laws behind sailing. These laws also apply to air travel.

When the trip was over, the record was broken! The trip took 69 days and 19 hours. Rich and Bill

Kidnet

wrote in to thank Prodigy's kids for rooting for them and cheering them on. Many kids who had followed the trip through Prodigy were waiting for Bill and Rich when they landed in Boston harbor!

Prodigy maintains the online area even though the trip is over. The ship's logs and the planned activities remain interesting, and who knows? They may even try to break their own record with another trip!

Mountain Challenge (MOUNTAIN)
Mountain Challenge followed 88-year-old Norman Vaughan on an Antarctic adventure. The expedition is long over, but the information is still here. Your kids can learn about the technology, nutrition, navigation, and safety equipment necessary to explore the Antarctic. They can also take a fun little quiz helping Norman's dogs pack their bags for the trip, and testing their knowledge of surviving in the Antarctic.

THE INTERNET

The World Wide Web
Stewart Brand of Whole Earth Catalog fame recently wrote in Time Magazine that for the generation of the 60s, geodesic domes and LSD didn't "work" but computers live on as valuable tools for change. He may be right. Read on.

EnviroWeb
(http://envirolink.org./)

This is one of the best places to begin exploring the Net's environmental resources. There are details on green products, and a link to a Virtual Environmental Library that includes an environmental activism section. Here your kids will find details on causes they can get involved in (e.g., saving Ecuadorian Rain Forests). One of EnviroWeb's more interesting features is an EnviroArts Gallery where users can post essays, photographs, and (eventually) poetry and examples of musical and sound expressions. Like many sites, this was under construction.

Solstice
(http://solstice.crest.org/)

Solstice is the place to turn for information about renewable energy and sustainable technology (solar energy, solar cells, wind energy). It's from CREST, the Center for Renewable Energy and Sustainable Technology, based in Washington, DC (see Figure 10.7). From here you can get to other information-rich sites such as the Department of Energy's Energy Efficiency and Renewable Energy Network.

Figure 10.7 Solstice WWW Home Page

USING SOLSTICE

(By Andrew Waegel, Internet Services Mgr., Center for Renewable Energy and Sustainable Technology)

As for how kids can best use our site, they probably can say better than I can! What I imagine, though, is that our site is a great, non-intimidating environment in which they can learn at their own pace, outside the regimented environment of a classroom. Hopefully, kids would feel like they can ask questions via this same "comments" channel that you used without the intimidation that might accompany talking to an expert in person.

Kids often feel more comfortable with this technology than older folks and perhaps see it as a more "normal" way to find out about things. I'd like to ask some of our younger visitors to see if this is true.

We've had several requests for more information in specific areas from kids involved in science fairs wanting to know where to get PV cells for their project; which I think is a GREAT use of the service (Especially if I can get a good answer to them)!

Eventually, I'd like to develop the potential of Solstice to foster connections between groups of people rather than serving as a simple receptacle of content. These could be professional groups (we run a bioenergy mailing list now, which is a good example of this idea). Perhaps we could have a service that focuses on students and renewable/sustainable development, either in an individual way (like a mailing list) or in a collective way (a class home page illustrating their project/research/etc).

The Jason Project
(http://seawifs.gsfc.nasa.gov/JASON/HTML/JASON_HOME.html)

The Jason Project was begun in 1989 by Dr. Robert D. Ballard, who received thousands of letters from kids wanting to know how he discovered the remains of the RMS Titanic. Since then, an annual two-week expedition is held; the goings-on are "broadcast in real time to a network of educational, research, and cultural institutions using state-of-the-art technology." Here are some of the expeditions the project has taken:

- Examined an ancient Roman shipwreck and retrieved artifacts from 2100 feet of water. Students used a two-way satellite audio system to question expedition scientists as they worked.
- A comprehensive examination of two perfectly preserved War of 1812 warships that had been on the bottom of Lake Ontario since 1813.
- Traveled to the Central American country of Belize to study the health of planet earth and the effect people have on our planet. Scientists explored life in the canopy of a rain forest and the largest barrier reef in the Western Hemisphere during live broadcasts.

Through "telepresence", students and educators worldwide can join the expedition. Telepresence involves the use of satellites to beam the goings-on to "interactive sites" where students see the research as it's being conducted.

Students can even remotely control hi-tech land rovers (the kind used for moon explorations). Fascinating.

ExploraNet
(http://www.exploratorium.edu/)

The Exploratorium is a hands-on science museum located in the Palace of Fine Arts in San Francisco's Marina District. If you live in the area, or are just visiting, check it out. Otherwise, this site gives you a good feel for the museum's approach, and the Internet's potential as a learning tool.

If you click on the Digital Library link you can play with digital versions of some of the museum's exhibits. Shown in Figure 10.8 is Bird in A Cage, an optical illusion that demonstrates that if you stare at something long enough you'll start to see things that aren't really there!

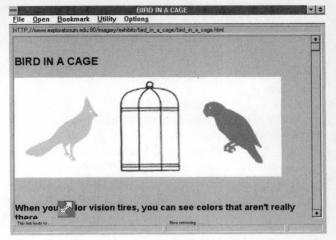

Figure 10.8 "Bird in a Cage"—a digital exhibit from the Exploratorium

Parents who are into science, or just looking for science fair ideas, should look into the Exploratorium's Science Snackbook link. It's direct address is: http//www.exploratorium.edu/papers/snackbook/snackbook.html

It features complete instructions for building classroom versions of many of the Exploratorium's exhibits.

Stay tuned: the Exploratorium's Webmaster told us he had lots of plans for adding more to the site!

VolcanoWorld
(http://volcano.und.nodak:edu/vw.html)
Especially geared to students, through this site kids can pose questions to a volcanologist. The site also has images of volcanoes, information about becoming a volcanologist, and astronauts' photos of volcanoes. There's even an area devoted to volcano-related toys!

A Tourist's Expedition to Antarctica
(http://http2.sils.umich.edu/Antartica/Story.html)

This describes the experiences of a cruise of the MV Marco Polo to Antarctica. It was a nominee in the Best of Web '94 awards. There are personal journal entries, photographs, and audio recordings. This web site is from the University of Michigan's school of education.

University of California Museum of Paleontology
(http://ucmp1.berkeley.edu/)
Learn how to become a PaleoPal—a service by which your child can pose any question concerning an aspect of paleontology and get an answer online.

EcoWeb
(http://ecosys.drdr.virginia.edu/EcoWeb.html)
From the University of Virginia, EcoWeb has some information specific to the university's recycling programs, but also resources of more general interest. Its links to other environmental resources on the Internet are its best feature. These include a link to the EcoGopher, through which you can get listings of environmental groups and programs in the U.S. A search capability called Katie lets you search "all text in all ecosystems." We plugged in the term "solar energy" and found more than a dozen articles of interest.

The Franklin Institute Science Museum
(http://sln.fi.edu/)
One of Philadelphia's great museums, The Franklin Institute has been a popular school trip destination for decades. This site emphasizes providing starting points that teachers, students, parents, and children can use to begin their own explorations (see Figure 10.9). An example of the "inquiry-based" study modules you'll find here is "Wind: Our Fierce Friend." It's packed with resources that support a hands-on investigation of wind. New online exhibits will cover weather and the brain.

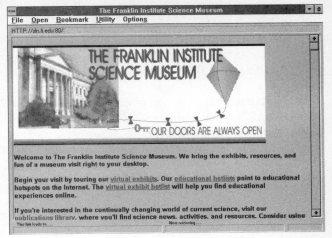

Figure 10.9 The Franklin Institute WWW Home Page

Newsgroups

Your budding activist will find many kindred spirits on the Internet's newsgroups. Ecology-related newsgroups don't generate as much traffic as some others, but the chatter is inspiring and pointed. Some of these discussions may be too advanced for younger kids.

As you might expect, discussion on alt.save.the. earth ranged from whalers, to the killing of elephants for ivory, the slaughter of seals, to the overpopulation of the earth. We did spot a rather rude, obscenity-filled diatribe, but that's probably not the norm here.

On talk.environment one message subject read: Save the Environment? You Must! This is the busiest of the environment-related newsgroups.

Sci.bio.ecology featured research on ecological subjects including solar energy, tropical biology, endangered animals, and fieldwork in Borneo.

On sci.bio.evolution the buzz was about from whence we came. Desmond Morris lives!

People into the biology of amphibians and reptiles show up in sci.bio.herp. A breeder of corn snakes was able to get some specific advice about what he needed to cross to get a desired species. Wow! Someone else was looking for sources of information on Gila Monsters. He was referred to the classic book on the topic "The Gila Monster and Its Allies." So there.

Sci.geo.meteorology is the place to discuss tornadoes, humidity, dewpoint, wind-chill factors, and understanding the other stuff that happens outside your windows. This newsgroup gets some traffic from kids. We found a posting from a child asking about the warming of the Eastern half of the U.S.

THE BEST OF THE REST

eWorld
The Tech Museum of Innovation (TECH MUSEUM)

Based in San Jose, CA, the heart of the Silicon Valley, the Tech Museum of Innovation was listed as one of the top 10 new tourist sites for 1990. It has six types of interactive exhibits: microelectronics, space exploration, high-tech bikes, robotics, materials, and bio-technology. The online area is something of an advertisement right now, but if you're planning a trip to the museum, bring your kids here first to plan your visit.

11

Pets and Other Animals

If your kids love animals they'll find plenty of company online. Pet lovers live in every corner of cyberspace, and they love to talk about their pets! This is probably the chattiest group of cybernauts you'll meet. They sincerely want to know the species, breed, color, and personal habits of your animals. If your kids are working on training a new pup or trying to find out what's wrong with an aging cat, why not send them online to talk with vets, breeders, and other pet lovers?

AMERICA ONLINE

Pet Care Forum (PETS)

A division of the Veterinary Information Network, Inc., the Pet Care Forum (see Figure 11.2) is staffed by an enormous group of people just waiting to answer your child's pet questions. The staff includes veterinarians from all over the country who specialize in everything from dogs to birds to fish to animal cardi-

Figure 11.1 Downloaded via Internet from wuarchive.wustl.edu

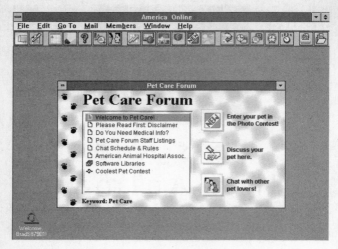

Figure 11.2 Pet Care Forum on America Online

ology and pharmacology. You will also find breeders, groomers, animal rights activists, and passionate pet owners (and that's just the staff!).

The message board includes nine categories for discussion. When we were there, there were 93,474 messages, so you can see these folks are busy. Show your child how to use the *Find Since* icon. This will show her only the messages that have been posted since the date she specifies. It's a good way to reduce the number of messages she'll have to scroll through. On subsequent visits, she can click on *Find New* and only those messages posted since her last visit will appear.

The libraries are chock full of files on every imaginable pet subject. You can search by species or breed or problem-behavior. Dozens of .GIFs let you find images of your favorite species and breed. You will also find information galore about different breeds, their standards, and the training necessary to make them competitive. Chat files capture the logs of live chats and store them for the visitors who missed them.

COMPUSERVE

Pet Forum (PETSONE)

By the time you read this, the Pet forum will have its own monthly newsletter. Members can submit .GIF files, stories, poems, or articles that would interest other pet owners. This forum is the place where owners of more traditional pets hang out. It's long been a favorite of ours.

When the groomer broke our puppy's back leg, she told us it was just a routine accident that can easily happen when you deal with puppies. Well, we dropped into the Pet forum and asked those folks what they thought. Within about six hours we'd heard from four vets and three groomers. They all agreed that not only was this not a routine accident, but none of them had ever heard of such a thing!

They gave us loads of advice about getting the medical help Bear needed, and they offered some suggestions about what we could do in dealing with the groomer. Some of those suggestions can't be repeated in a book meant for parents and kids g, but with the information we gathered, we went to the groomer's boss. You may be able to guess that the groomer paid every penny of the $200 + medical bills. Happily, Bear is as good as new, and snoring under the desk right now. Not only did we get this valuable and usable information when we needed it, but we also got countless messages from pet lovers who saw our note and wanted to offer some comfort. These were priceless to our family as we got through this little ordeal. The same type of help and support is waiting for your kids, too.

Your kids will find library files about dogs, cats, and birds. The library includes a Writers' Corner where people are encouraged to submit their original work on the subject of their pets. The Writers' Corner is especially interesting (okay, so it was to us), because it includes stories for kids that forum members have written about their pets.

Animals Forum (PETSTWO)

The Animals forum is about all the other kinds of animals people keep or love; from snakes to spiders to bats and guinea pigs (see Figure 11.3). Your kids will find message boards and libraries that include Ask-A-Shoer (to get in touch with a farrier, you know, someone who puts shoes on horses), Pets International, and Insects and Arachnids.

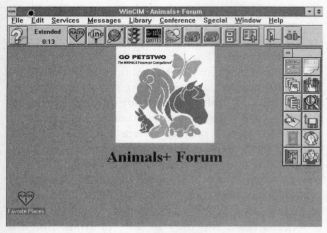

Figure 11.3 The Animals Forum on CompuServe

Aquaria/Fish Forum (FISHNET)

Here's the place to be if your kids have a little bit of the undersea world in their lives. They'll get answers to their questions, help with their problems, and advice on keeping their undersea pets alive and well. Staff members include scientists and experienced hobbyists. The annual Winter Weekend Workshop is an event that includes conferences, lectures, auctions, and contests for fish lovers. The folks here are serious about their aquaria fun, but no doubt this friendly group would welcome your serious young fish enthusiast, too (see Figure 11.4).

Figure 11.4 Downloaded via Internet from wuarchive.wustl.edu

Dinosaur Forum (DINOFORUM)

Okay, so your kid probably doesn't have a dinosaur, but let's not quibble. Most childhoods include at least some fascination with these ancient creatures. The Dinosaur forum members discuss every aspect of the study of dinosaurs, including the role dinosaurs play in today's popular culture (see Figure 11.5). The libraries are stuffed full of .GIFs to delight every species of dinosaur lover. As a matter of fact, graphic images are so important to this forum that there is even a graphics tutorial to make it easy for you to learn about graphic files in general and those in the Dinosaur forum's libraries in particular.

A special section of the message board and libraries is devoted to DinoKids. When we visited, a conference for 4- to 9-year-olds was just getting started. You'll find ongoing dinosaur mystery quizzes, dinosaur jokes, and kids who are actually digging around for dinosaur fossils in their own neighborhoods.

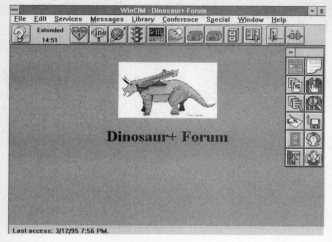

Figure 11.5 The Dinosaur Forum on CompuServe

Pets News Clips (PETNEWS) ($)

Here are news stories from the animal world. Your kids can check out clips from the major news wires relating to all types of animals. Stories include coverage of significant events of the day, plus animal rights activities and scientific discoveries relating to both living and extinct species.

PRODIGY

Petcare Guide (PETCARE)

This is a collection of articles written by vets for the lay person. The articles are endorsed by the Humane Society of the U.S. Subjects range from teaching children humane treatment of animals, to caring for sick pets, to keeping wolves as pets (the word is, don't do it!).

Pets BB (PETS BB) (+)

Like the other forums we've already talked about, this one is full of people who love animals. What makes this one a little different, is that it includes a

Kidnet

topic area specifically for kids. When we visited, there was a very elaborate imaginary horse show going on. Kids participated by posting messages, usually under assumed names, about breeding and racing their imaginary horses. Of course, there were also plenty of messages from kids who really did have horses, too!

Another interesting message thread was from the Animal Lovers Club. This group is dedicated to trying to stop animal testing of products. Although visitors are free to discuss any animal, according to BB veterans, only the horse clubs last for more than a few months.

THE INTERNET

The World Wide Web

Have a pet, or thinking of getting one? You can bet there's a Web site or maybe even a dozen or more devoted to it. Here's a sampling of what we found. We've listed the topics and the number of distinct Web sites next to it:

Beekeeping (6)
Birds (11)
Cats (19)
Cows (2)
Dogs (46)
Ferrets (6)
Fish (18)
Herpetology (16)

Horses (2)
Lemurs (6)
Marsupials (1)
Rabbits (2)
Sheep (1)
Squid (1)!
Whales (1)

The Animal Information Data Base
(http://www.bev.net/education/SeaWorld/infobook.html)

Look no further than this site, from Sea World and Busch Gardens, for your animal facts (see Figure 11.6). We thought this would be little more than an electronic ad, but we were pleasantly surprised. Children can learn about animals from the African Lion

File   Open   Bookmark   Utility   Options

HTTP://www.bev.net.80/education/SeaWorld/infobook.html

Animal Information Data Base

Based on a long-term commitment to education, Sea World and Busch Gardens strive to provide an enthusiastic, imaginative, and intellectually stimulating atmosphere to help students reach their academic potential. Specifically our goals are...

- To instill in students of all ages an appreciation for science and a respect for all living creatures and natural environments.
- To conserve our valuable natural resources by increasing awareness of the interrelationships of humans and the environment.
- To increase students' basic competencies in science and other disciplines.
- To provide an educational resource for the entire community.

The ocean and its inhabitants fascinate us, and this fascination leads to a quest for

This link leads to ...   Now retrieving ...

Figure 11.6 The Animal Information Database (Sea World, Busch Gardens) WWW Home Page

to the Walrus in a special "Animal Bytes" section. Kids will especially like the fun facts that are included (e.g., an adult lion's roar can be heard up to five miles away and warns off intruders or reunites scattered pride members). Aside from these information bytes, there are more complete Information Booklets available on Baleen Whales, Bottlenose Dolphins, Corals and Coral Reefs, Gorillas, Manatees, Killer Whales, and Walruses.

Pet Pages
(http://sashimi.wwa.com/~-tenec/users/paulf/pets/pets.html)

On Pet Pages you may find a picture of your own pet one day (see Figure 11.7). All you have to do is put it there. Complete instructions are included. There are categories for dogs, cats, and other animals. In addition to the picture, you can include some inside information on what your pet is like and "the story behind the picture." There are also some links here to other "pet " places of interest.

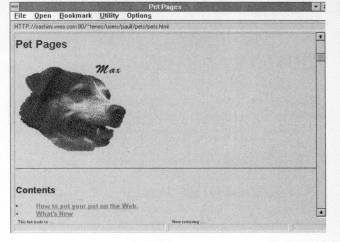

Figure 11.7 Pet Pages WWW Home Page

The Krib
(http://marge.phys.washington.edu./fish/)

Fish fiends will want to check out "The Krib"—an excellent collection of pages devoted to aquariums and tropical fish. There are handy links to newsgroup postings, as well as some original articles that you won't find elsewhere.

Cats on the Internet
(http://http2.sils.umich.edu/~-dtorres/cats/cats.html)

Cat lovers love to tell you about their pets and show you their pictures. Cat lovers who are on the Internet are no exception. The "Cats on the Internet" page was designed to provide links to World Wide Web pages that cat owners have created to feature pictures and information about their pets (see Figure 11.8). Many of the pages created by the cat lovers provide links to other cat-related resources and pages available on the Internet. "Cats on the Internet" was created mainly for the pleasure of reading about other people's pets, but there's also an educational benefit. For example, one link is to the "Cat Fanciers'

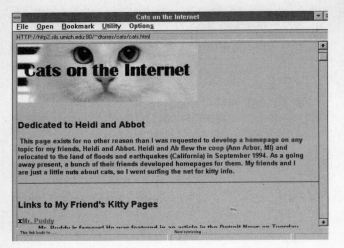

Figure 11.8 Cats on the Internet WWW Home Page

Home Page" which contains lots of information about cat breeds.

"Cats on the Internet" is maintained by a doctoral student at the School of Information and Library Studies at the University of Michigan.

The Dog WWW Page
(http://www.sdsmt.edu./other/dogs/dog.html)

With more than 40 sites devoted to dogs, there's a fairly good chance you'll find a site devoted to your special breed. German Shepherds, Chihuahuas, Golden Retrievers, Bulldogs, and Collies are some of those with their sites.

Start with the Dog WWW Site where you can get information on AKC breeds, and very detailed answers to frequently asked questions including topics likely to interest kids, such as *Your New Puppy/Dog.*

Birding on the Web
(http://compstat.wharton.upenn.edu:8001/~-siler/birding.html)

This is a remarkably complete resource that's a model of its type. If your child has even a remote interest in birds, we recommend this site as a way to feed this interest. It features lists of books, videos, and CD-ROMs, and loads of FAQs. A separate bird chat area includes mail received by the bird hotline. A peek at the mail found notices of various bird sightings.

The Froggy Page
(http://haskell.cs.yale.edu/sjl/www/skater-images/
frogs/frogs-on-ice.html)
For a completely frivolous but fun site we recommend The Froggy Page, which "contains links to froggy things from various places on the net." There are plenty of frog pictures here, frog sounds you can sample, frog stories such as The Toad Princess by Grimm, and Frog Fables from Aesop. All this is brought to you by that frog-friendly university, Yale.

Newsgroups
Your kids will find plenty of useful information posted on the pet-related newsgroups. Kids should feel free to post here; but as usual they should read the associated FAQ files first. There's little flaming—just people talking about critters. Occasionally, vets answer the questions that are posed.

POSTING FROM THE REC.PETS.CATS NEWSGROUP

Question: Do the great cats—tigers, lions, and leopards—purr?

Response: (posted an hour later) None of the large cats—tigers, lions, leopards, or jaguars—has the ability to purr. Their vocal structure is different than that of the small cats. Tigers have the ability to make a sound called a chuff. Tigers chuff when greeting, or when they are scared and trying to reassure themselves. I have trained tigers, lions, and cougars for over 17 years and have only heard cougars purr, which is very loud."

On rec.birds we found birders talking about binoculars and what to feed robins (they'll reportedly "kill" for a blueberry.) A 9-year-old about to leave on a vacation with his parents to Switzerland, wanted to know whether he could expect to do some serious birding during the trip.

We checked out rec.pets and it seemed just fine for kids. Lurk for a bit to get the tone of the group before posting.

Examples of other pet and animal newsgroups are:

- alt.pets.hamsters
- alt.pets.rabbits
- rec.equestrian
- rec.pets.cats
- rec.pets.dogs.breeds
- rec.pets.herp

THE BEST OF THE REST

eWorld
Pets & Animals Forum (PETS)
This area is sponsored by Pets in Need, a non-profit animal adoption agency. Here, your kids will find the usual bulletin board. When we checked, it wasn't very active, but we did find a long thread about horses, which we're sure our daughter, Stephanie, would want to check out. The Animal House area included some files on pet care and training, and pictures of people's pets.

12

International
Cultures

More than anything else, online travel opens your home to people from all over the world and their cultures. If your child never gains anything else from being online, except the friendship of one individual from a distant land, your online experiment will be a success. Of course, he will gain many other things, but it's very possible that a long-term friendship with someone entirely different will be what means the most to him. Opportunities for this type of friendship abound, and this chapter will lead you to them.

AMERICA ONLINE

The International House (IES) (T)

The International House is part of the Interactive Education Services (IES) section of America Online. We didn't cover the IES because its services are more appropriate to college and graduate students than they are to younger kids. Still, the International House is an old off-campus tradition—a place where

Figure. 12.1 Downloaded via Internet from sunsite.unc.edu

people can gather and share their cultures, holidays, and world views. One of the International House's features is a nightly live conference in a foreign language. There is a lot of serious study going on here, but there is also a lot of cultural give and take and holiday celebrations too.

Corbis Media (CORBIS)
Continuum Productions Corporation provides commercial users with access to the world's largest digital collection of fine imagery. Corbis Media is a division of Continuum Productions, and the creator of this forum on America Online, which is used to introduce potential customers to its archive. The name, Corbis, is from the Latin word meaning "woven basket." Into this woven basket Corbis has placed an amazing collection of images that you can download and use at no extra charge. The only stipulation is that you use the images for research or for personal enjoyment. So, if your child wants one for a school report or just because they're cool, that wouldn't be a problem.

Among the images available, you will find a Thai Temple Dancer, a Beefeater from the Tower of London, or a Guatemalan street vendor, to name just a few. File libraries are organized by geographic area so that you may search all of the images available from Europe, or Asia, or the Americas.

COMPUSERVE

In addition to the forums discussed below, there are many other subject-specific forums. If your child is interested in African-American culture, for example, you'll find an African-American Arts and Culture forum. These forums are not geared toward children, but you would certainly be welcome to "take" your child into any forum on CompuServe and judge it for yourself.

World Community Forum (EWCFORUM)

This forum is unlike any other place we found online (see Figure 12.2). It is devoted to worldwide communications across language barriers. It uses sophisticated translation software to post messages in English, French, German, and Spanish. Here's how it works.

Actually, we're talking about four separate forums. When you sign on, you join in the forum of your native language. Every message you post is automatically translated and posted in the three other forums! The result is fascinating, because every message that gets translated into English also includes the message in the language in which it was originally written.

The translation software is not exact, and that leads to some charming expressions. For example, "Do you have seen the interesting translation, the message out of Washington, Direct Current (DC)?" As you can see, it's good enough for you or your kids to understand everything posted. It's also fun to look through the original message to try and decipher some of it on your own. The thought of translation software is most amazing. Just imagine when this technology advances

Fig. 12.2 The World Community Forum on CompuServe

to the point where language is no longer a barrier to any of our international communication!

One section of the message board is devoted to kids, and here you will find the usual requests for key-pals and exchanges of opinions about music, sports, and school. Every week there is a live conference in the forum for kids to meet and chat in realtime.

Living History Forum (LIVING)

If your child is interested in the cultures of other times as well as other places, drop into this forum where the past meets the present (see Figure 12.3). Forum members are dedicated to the study of history, archaeology, and the cultures and mores of times past. Many of them are historical re-enactors, and you'll find members of groups like the Society for Creative Anachronism.

These folks aren't satisfied to just think about history, they work hard to create living experiences of history! Your kids can stop here to get a very personal view of history. Whether it is discussing the minutiae of past battles or creating an authentic Medieval cos-

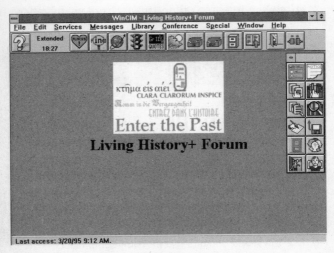

Fig. 12.3 The Living History Forum on CompuServe

tume, your kids will get a different perspective on history and your history buffs will have found Nirvana!

In 1994 the movie *Little Women* brought the past to life for many of us. We used the Living History forum on CompuServe to plan a Victorian birthday party for a 10-year-old girl. We went in search of recipes, game ideas, and decorations that would put us right back in the 19th Century.

Our first message response suggested that we make simple long skirts for the girls and vests for the boys, to make them feel more "oldtime." We should play quoits, but the old-fashioned way with rings of rope. Had we thought of a taffy pull? Most kids this age would be willing to give it a try. If the party was for girls only (as lots of them are at this age), the girls might like to make sachets. Directions for gathering the supplies and putting them together followed.

The next message told us about decorations. First, crepe paper streamers and designs cut from paper would give the room a Victorian feel. We should also use lacy paper doilies everywhere, as placemats and under the table's centerpiece. The last touch would be to decorate the table with nosegays or tussie mussies, one for each guest, again wrapped in lace doilies.

Finally, we heard from a student in England working on a degree on the history of the Victorian Period. He told us of two books, *The Victorian Child* and *Victorian Entertainment*. He assured us that we'd find everything else we might need in these two publications, and he gave us all the information we'd need to locate them. He signed his message with the wish, "May you and your family be well and happy always."

Cook's Forum (COOKS)

What, you say your kids don't cook? Well, ours don't either, but who doesn't love to eat. After checking in with people from all over the world, your kids might just get curious about what people in other countries eat and how they cook it. Or, take the initiative yourself. If your child makes a new distant keypal, why not take him over to Cook's Forum and search out a favorite recipe from his keypal's homeland? His friendship will take on a new dimension by tasting the foods that are familiar to his friend, and your encouragement will reinforce to him how important it is to look at the world (and taste it) from someone else's viewpoint.

Foreign Language Forum (FLEFO)

This forum is such a storehouse of valuable knowledge and experience about foreign languages, that we debated whether it should go in this chapter or the School chapter. Yes, your kids can get all the help they'll need with their foreign language studies (even if they're studying Turkish), but beyond that, this is an extraordinary place to meet people from every corner of the earth.

The first time we dropped in, we found a message from a first-time forum visitor—a Korean high-school student living in New York. He was homesick and lonely for people who speak his native language. Within 24 hours, he had received a message from another young Korean man living in the U.S. It seems that on his first visit, he discovered the homesick message, and the two became instant keypals.

Religion Forum (RELIGION) (T)

"We are primarily a discussion forum whose main purpose is to provide an opportunity for people from many different religious traditions and from none, to share their thoughts, ideas, beliefs, practices, and customs with each other in open discussion and debate." The Religion Forum is a serious place. Your younger kids won't care at all what's here, but your older ones may want to learn more about the religious backgrounds of the many different friends

Fig. 12.4 Downloaded via Internet from wuarchive.wustl.edu

they'll meet online. They can come here and ask any question about human religious expression they can think of. As long as the question is asked respectfully, informative and friendly answers will flow back to them (see Figure 12.4).

There is a section of the message board, Youth Line, devoted to young members. These are more likely high schoolers than junior high schoolers. They discuss issues ranging from the worst date they've ever had to homosexuality and prayer in school. The discussions, although mature, are respectful and lively. Your child's curiosity may very well lead to questions about other religions that you can't answer. If so, you know where to take him.

PRODIGY

Ask Beth

Advice columns have always been popular, and *Ask Beth* offers advice specifically to kids. We think it gives kids a chance to look into their peers' heads and maybe gain a new perspective, so we counted it as a cultural feature of Prodigy. The advice columnist known to millions as *Ask Beth* is really Elizabeth Winship, mother of four and honors graduate of Radcliffe College. Every Tuesday and Friday Beth posts answers to questions Prodigy users ask. If she chooses your question to answer, she will delete your name and ID to protect your privacy.

While working in a CompuServe forum, we met a young man who called himself Fly. He's from Newcastle, England, and he shared with us some of the dialect people use in his part of the country. That dialect is called Geordie. Although we still have never actually heard the words spoken, thanks to Fly, we know a little bit more about how people in northern England sound!

Hi Deb, Fly here, I'm really called Chris. The title is translated as "learn yourself Geordie." I am going to give you some of the Geordie anthem. Anyone from Newcastle knows this song.

LARN YA SEL GEORDIE

Aw went te Blaydon Races, 'twas on the ninth of Joon,
Eiteen hundred an' sixty two, on a summer's efternoon,
Aw teuk the' bus frae Balmbra's, an' she was heavy laden,
Away we went alang Collingwood Street, that's on the
    road te Blaydon
Chorus:
O lads, ye should only see us gannon,
We passe the foaks upon the road just as they were
    stannin;
Thor we lots o' lads an' lasses there, all wi smiling faces,
Gan alang the Scotswood Road, to see the Blaydon Races.

Newcastle's a pretty cool city. We are situated next to a river, there is a cathedral and all the usual, I s'pose you'd like it. See ye lyater leek, bye!

We s'pose Fly's right, we would like it!

THE INTERNET

The World Wide Web

Some of the world's great museums are just a mouse click away thanks to the Internet. If your household is too busy to get to a museum, Internet access takes away the last of your excuses for not going. The doors are always open for electronic field trips.

At the time of this writing, plans were being developed for the Internet 1996 World Exposition, a world's fair of sorts that will take place on the Internet. Use Yahoo or Webcrawler to search for the associated sites.

City.Net
(http://www.city.net/)

In this one place, City.Net provides tourist information and pictures for thousands of places. You can search for a particular place by clicking on a spot on the world map that's here, or you can search the database directly by entering a city or country.

Is it any easier to use this than to just pick up an atlas or encyclopedia? Certainly not. But City.Net is much more fun, probably more up to date, and the hyperlinking encourages browsing.

Travels With Samantha
(http://www.swiss.ai.mit.edu/samantha/travels-with-samantha.html)

A Best of Web '94 winner, this is a virtual travelogue "about the summer I spent seeing North America, meeting North Americans, and trying to figure out how people live," says guide Philip Greenspun.

Highlights of the trip include:

Both sides of the language war in Montreal
Bored youths in the Midwest
Struggling single mothers in the Yukon
Free Spirits in Alaska
Polygamists in Salt Lake City

Oh yes: Samantha is Greenspun's traveling companion—a Macintosh Powerbook notebook computer. Your kids should read this for the writing and the escapist appeal. The pictures may be great, but they can take quite a while to download.

World Arts Resources
(http://www.cgrg.ohio-state.edu/Newark/artsres.html)

This site attempts to provide, in one handy place, links to all of the Net's major arts resources. What an arts bonanza! You'll find links to:

- Museums: More than 150 from just the U.S.
- Art Galleries and Exhibitions: More than 160 Resources
- Art Publications: Over 30
- Institutions and "Government" Resources: Over 40

EXPO Ticket Office
(http://wunsite.unc.edu/expo/ticket_office.html)

When your kids walk through these virtual doors they can visit the Vatican, Soviet archives only recently made public, the Dead Sea Scrolls exhibit, and a paleontology exhibit. When they're finished, have them stop by the EXPO restaurant, which features masterpieces of French cookery.

The Smithsonian
(http://www.si.edu/)

Stop by here before planning a trip to any of the Smithsonian museums, including the Smithsonian Institute, the National Air and Space Museum, The Freer Gallery of Art and the Arthur M. Sackler Gallery, the Harvard-Smithsonian Center for Astrophysics, the National Museum of American Art, the National Museum of Natural History, and several others. Through this site, kids can also access research catalogs maintained by SI libraries, archives, and research units. These archives feature information about books, serials,

Fig. 12.5 Smithsonian Institution WWW Home Page

manuscripts, films, sound recordings, and paintings. Eventually, the treasures from "the nation's attic" will be available to all via the Internet (see Figure 12.5).

See the USA in Your Virtual Chevrolet
(http://www.std.com/NE/usatour.html)
   A compelling page of links, by state, to a wide variety of resources. Here's a sampling:

- California: Visit SurfNet for details on surfing worldwide, Dudes.
- Florida: Check out the Very Unofficial Guide to Walt Disney World.
- Hawaii: Read The Moon Travel Handbook "a guide to the sites and sounds of the Big Island."
- Kentucky: See photos of past Derby winners.
- Vermont: Find out how a whale wound up buried in Vermont in the University of Vermont's online exhibit.

The Human-Languages Page
(http://www.willamette.edu/~-tjones/Languages-Page.html)

This is a large site devoted to bringing together information about the world's languages. It's meant for an older audience, but even younger kids can appreciate the language lessons available (especially in Spanish and Italian). There are various English to/from-another-language dictionaries; some are more complete than others.

Newsgroups

Search listings using the keyword "culture" or "arts," and you'll find scores of newsgroups ranging from alt.culture.argentina to alt.culture.zippies. These can make for fascinating reading for your budding cultural anthropologist. While one day these may be useful places to pose questions relating to school assignments, for now kids are better off using services specifically set up for that sort of thing, such as CompuServe's World Community Forum.

THE BEST OF THE REST

Delphi
The Dictionary of Cultural Literacy
This is a simple-to-use online version of Houghton Mifflin's Dictionary of Cultural Literacy. Enter a word, name, or phrase that has something to do with our culture, and you'll get a brief description of it. For example, we entered Rock, expecting a description of Rock & Roll. A menu of five likely matches including Rock-A-Bye Baby and Nelson Rockefeller appeared. Of course, Rock & Roll was a choice too. The definition included a brief discussion of the origins of Rock & Roll, a listing of some of the most famous Rock stars, and a menu of related references for pursuing our search further. The copyright date for this information is 1988, and you can tell that it's old. We tried to find Jim Carrey, Smashing Pumpkins, and Kurt Cobain and the database didn't recognize any of these.

Kidnet

13

Humor

Some people don't think that computers or the people who use them could possibly be funny. Well, they're wrong. Sometimes we burst out laughing just because we think funny things. Did you hear the one about the guy and his dog who went into the computer store. . . Okay, okay, we'll get back to work. Hop online to track down your favorite cartoon or comic strip. You'll be surprised how much laughter is possible through a modem.

AMERICA ONLINE

Cartoons (CARTOONS)
The Cartoons area includes libraries filled with cartoons and comics. These folks are serious about producing funny stuff. A lot of what your kids will find here was created on computers. There's plenty of information in the Cartoons area to tell your kids exactly how to download and view the cartoons.

Cartoon Network (CARTOON NETWORK)
This is the online home of the Cartoon Network. We can personally testify that the cartoon has not lost its

Fig. 13.1 Downloaded via Internet from wuarchive.wustl.edu

appeal. As much as we may want you to think our kids prefer only educational programming, if you ask them, they want cartoons! And lots of them! The folks at the Cartoon Network must have known that when they went online.

The welcome screen is bright and dynamic; you'd think it was designed for kids! Rather than list items in the standard menu form, each portion of the online service is represented by a colorful icon (see Figure 13.2).

Click on Elroy Jetson, for example, and you'll pull up a menu describing the Cartoon Network and offering daily, monthly, and weekend program listings and Network press releases. Click on Moxy's picture and pull up everything you could want to know about the Network's official "spokestoon."

When we visited, the Cartoon Network was promising an upcoming Hanna-Barbera section, including information and artwork from such well-loved cartoons, as the Flintstones and the Jetsons. World Premiere Toons focuses on the weekly airing of

Fig. 13.2 The Cartoon Network on America Online

48 seven-minute cartoons produced by Hanna-Barbera and the Cartoon Network.

The message board is full of chatter from kids and grown-ups who just love cartoons. Some of the messages posted were from kids as young as four, and some were obviously from grown-ups who loved the cartoons when they were four! This seems like a fun place for your cartoon fans to hang out without too much worry about who they'll bump into or what they'll stumble upon.

The Studio is the Cartoon Network's live chat area. When we visited, the Network was planning to schedule monthly conferences with professional animators, cartoon characters, and Network administrators. When no conference is scheduled, members are free to gather together for live chats.

The Toon Boutique is the Cartoon Network's online boutique where visitors can shop for t-shirts, mugs, backpacks, caps, and more, featuring their favorite Cartoon Network stars.

Comedy Central (COMEDY)

This is the forum for the cable network Comedy Central. Your kids will find descriptions of Comedy Central shows along with scheduling and ticket information. The message boards are for discussing Comedy Central programs and attitudes.

Nothing in this area is geared specifically toward kids. Much of it reflects the same attitude you'll find on Comedy Central. If you and your kids enjoy the kind of humor you find on Comedy Central, you'll get a hoot out of this online stop. If you find that type of humor offensive or objectionable, you'll want to wait till the kids are in bed before you log on.

COMPUSERVE

Comics/Animation Forum (COMICS) (T)

This forum is for fans of comic books, comic strips, and animation. Forum members discuss and debate the virtues and vices of their favorite comics and characters. The libraries are full of .GIFs. But, we must warn you, there are Adult Comic sections in the message board and libraries. Although your older kids will probably not find anything here that is worse than what they've already seen, we can't recommend you let your younger ones explore here without an escort.

PRODIGY

Punchline (PUNCHLINE)

If your kids are into corny humor, they'll be at home here. But they'll have to be into really corny humor, because some of this stuff is so bad you can still see the cobs! If they're always coming to you with really awful jokes, show them how to submit their worst (we mean their best g) to Punchline so they can see their names listed on-screen with their jokes.

Twisted Tales (TWISTED TALES)

This is the computer-age version of the old parlor

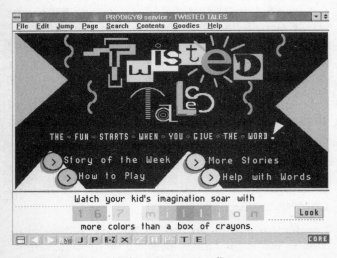

Fig. 13.3 The Twisted Tales Screen on Prodigy

game that asks you for a list of seemingly unrelated words (see Figure 13.3). The words then get plugged into blank spaces in a story. The result is ridiculous and sure to please. Every week a new story is featured, but your kids can also choose a story theme such as school, sports, and helpful hints. When they finish their stories, print them out to send off to the relatives. They'll really wonder about you then!

THE INTERNET

The World Wide Web

Internet surfers are a fun-loving lot, if the number of Web sites in the "Humor, Jokes, and Fun" categories is any indication. That's the good news. The bad news is that what passes for fun for most net surfers should not, in most parent's minds, pass for fun for the kids. If you're careful, you can find some fun (see Figure 13.4), but just be vigilant about what kinds of humor your kids search for on the Net.

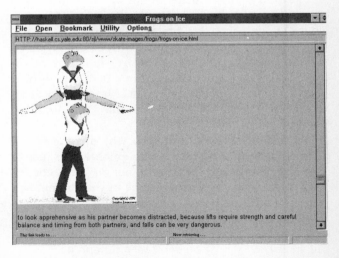

Fig. 13.4 Frogs On Ice from Figure Skating WWW Home Page

The great majority of these sites contain humor that's, well—sophomoric—which makes sense considering that so many college students use the Net. For example, there's a site called Blonde jokes (we didn't bother) and Bizarre sites (that's the name, we also passed). There were four sites devoted to lawyer jokes; as funny as some of them may have been we thought kids wouldn't get them. Worse yet, there was even a site devoted to Jeffrey Dahmer death jokes.

Comics 'n Stuff
(http://www.phlab.missouri.edu/HOMES/c617145–www/comix.html) (T)

For a quick overview of the funny stuff on the net, take a look at this site. It was voted a Best of the Web 1995 nominee at the time of our review.

Comics 'n Stuff claims to be the Internet equivalent of the newspaper funny pages. It provides links to general comics discussion areas such as alternative comics and comics and strips. In the comic cafe, fans can chat about the comic book industry. There are also many links to specific comics, such as Dilbert, NetBoy, and Marnie. Some of the comics you can get to may prove offensive, so watch for how your child is using this site. For example, The Jack T. Chick archive (didn't ring a bell with us either) had a warning next to it: "Catholics may find this offensive." The good thing about this site, and the only reason we feel we can even include it, is that at least it warns you about links you may not find kid friendly.

To be honest, we're not sure why anyone would read comics online when it's so much easier just to grab the newspaper. Admittedly, not all of the comics available on the net would also be in your hometown paper (that's probably a good thing). Remember, downloading images takes a lot longer than it does to download text, so unless you have a very fast modem (14.4 bps or 28.8 bps) we don't recommend it.

Welcome to Happily Ever After
(http://www.earthlink.net/~-heahome/)

Happily Ever After is a new comic strip about "the frog prince, his princess, and other fairy tale regulars (see Figure 13.5). The stories take place 15 years after that fateful kiss." This site, just getting underway when we visited, features sample strips, a link to the rec.arts.comics.strips newsgroup, and archives to past 'toons. Plans were in the works for a link to other "kid-acceptable" comics sites. As you can see from the sample shown here, the comic is mild enough to pass the parent test, but should still interest kids. The files also download quickly due to a special compression technique.

Fig. 13.5 A Sample Strip from Happily Ever After

The Calvin & Hobbes Comics Gallery
(http://infolabwww.kub.nl:2080/calvin_hobbes/index.html)

Calvin is the fun-loving boy and Hobbes is his toy tiger. Literally dozens of comics are here for the downloading. As the page says, "some of them are pretty big but they're definitely worth the wait."

Newsgroups

We can't recommend that kids hop on the Internet to find jokes or read discussions about comic strip heroes, characters, etc. Most of these sorts of discussions include a lot of stuff that your kids won't "get." We were also surprised that the relevant newsgroups (e.g., rec.humor.funny) had very little traffic.

THE BEST OF THE REST

GEnie
The Comics RoundTable (COMICS)
This is one of the busiest RoundTables on the service. There's plenty of information and conversation here that would interest any fan of comics. Topics open for discussion on the message boards include DC Comics, Marvel Comics, and Comics-Related Television.

14

Games

Kids today have access to the most sophisticated games ever known to humankind. Most of what you'll find online can't compare to what most kids can do with their hand-held or TV-based video games. Video games aside, there are so many software packages and CD-ROMs available for kids to play games on their computers, that whole books have been devoted to this subject alone. So, how can you best use online services to let your kids play games?

There are several ways. Your kids can play real-time, live interactive games. These take place online and can include just about anything: arcade-like games, classic board games, trivia, and word games, to name just a few. Some of these are tremendous fun. The fact that you can play with anyone from across the country or even across the world makes them even more exciting.

Your kids can also find software games galore to download and play offline. These games are usually shareware. Your kids can get them and play them for a while to decide if they like them. If they decide the games are "keepers," honor obliges you to pay the software author a registration fee for the program.

Figure 14.1 Downloaded via the Internet from wuarchive.ustl.edu

Usually, paying the fee is rewarded with another game or an enhanced version of the game you've already got. If you don't pay the registration fee, only you and your conscience will know. For the most part, programs you download will continue to be functional. Shareware games can be fast-paced, fun, educational, and inexpensive.

Look at the sidebar in the Internet section of this chapter for a list of some of the best shareware games available through the net. Many of these games are also available through the commercial services.

We like shareware games. Many of the games are very well produced and lots of fun to play. Your connect time charges only include the amount of time it takes to download the file, and you're sure to find something your kids will like. We'll focus a lot of attention in this chapter to finding and using shareware games.

Your kids can also go online to feed their video game habits. All the commercial services have forums for gamers. Your kids can go into these and find plenty of tips and hints for playing their Nintendo or Sega games. They can locate special codes, and they can exchange information and opinions with other people who play their favorite games.

The online world abounds with live-action, interactive games. Unlike shareware games that you download and play offline, interactive games are played online against real opponents. You may be surprised to learn that most of the people who play games online are not kids. You need to be vigilant, because the chances are very good that if your kids get involved with interactive online games, their opponents will be adults. This may not be a problem if your kids go online to challenge opponents in games of skill and luck. It can become a problem if youngsters get involved with adults and play role-playing, adventure, or multi-user games.

Kids can easily be overwhelmed in these and the distinction between fantasy and reality can confuse them. Therefore, we don't feel comfortable advising your kids start with these types of games. Let them get online and find some games to download. Encourage them to get to know other gamers online through the forums and message boards. This way, they'll gain experience and learn about online games. There's always time for them to pursue the role-playing, adventure, and multi-user games as they develop and hone their online skills.

AMERICA ONLINE

America Online puts game shareware together in one place, the Software Center, under the Computing hot button on the main menu. This makes it very easy to find and download them. Whether you use a DOS-based or Apple computer, you'll find software downloads work the same.

ETHAN FINDS A GAME

Ethan, age 7, asked if he could use America Online. We were working in the office at the time, and he's seen us use it so often, we figured it was okay. Boy, were we surprised when within five minutes he had downloaded XATAX (a shoot 'em up) all by himself. Here's the star downloader's account of how he did it.

I went on America Online. I looked under Computing. I chose Software Libraries. It said, "What do you want to look for?" I answered, "Games." I looked at all the games, and then I clicked on the game I wanted. It seemed like fun, because it said it had shooting in it. Then I got to the screen where it asked me where I wanted the file to go. I chose the place that was already there. Then it started getting the game!

By the way, when his dad told him this account would be in the book, Ethan said, "Wow—could you fix this game now?"

If you know the name of the file, just click on the Search the Libraries icon (see Figure 14.2). Next, you'll be prompted to enter which type of file you're looking for. You can search all the categories if you want, but the search will go much quicker if you know the name. Next, you'll see your search results. From this screen you can actually begin the download.

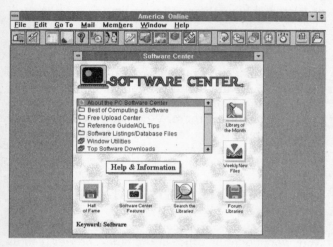

Figure 14.2 The Software Center Screen from America Online

If you don't know the name of your game, or if you just want to browse around a little, you have a couple of choices. The hot button, *Top Software Downloads*, will tell you what's hot, but it's not limited to just games. Select the *Best of Computing and Software* to get popular files, organized by categories, one of which is games. The *Hall of Fame* hot button will show you lists of games you may want to try. Among these are programs considered to be the best downloads for 1995, as recommended by forum leaders. Other categories include arcade games, best of games, and drawing for kids.

Kids Only (KIDS)

In the Kids Only section of America Online, you will find a hot button for *Games and Computers*. Pressing that button will call up a menu of programs that kids can download for playing offline. The categories of games include Kids Software, Children's Art Programs, and OS/2 Games.

The Kids Software section is heavy on screen puzzles. These puzzles show a complete picture that scrambles at the press of a button. Your child then has to use a mouse or the arrow keys to construct the complete picture again. These files are easy to download and require no special software or equipment to use them.

The Children's Art Programs range from stamp pads to electronic coloring programs to creative storymakers. They are more likely to require particular equipment to use, but they are also simple to download and with a little help, your kids can easily do it themselves.

The OS/2 files include games that run only on OS/2-based computers. They include such computer-based favorites as Hangman, SimCity, and Connect Four.

The Game Room

Your kids will find the Game Room under the *Online Games* hot button from the Games & Computers menu in America Online's Kids Only section. This is a live chat area where kids can meet to play games led by America Online staff members. The games are trivia and word games that require quick and clever thinking. Parents are invited to watch, but like most other parts of Kids Only, they are not welcome to participate. When we visited, the Game Room was open every day from 6:00 P.M. to 8:45 P.M. Eastern time. A different activity was planned for each night from Sunday through Friday. A quick check of the Game Room Calendar will tell you what is scheduled now, and you'll also find all the game playing rules on the same menu. This is a safe, well-supervised area for kids to go online for some fast-paced, live-action fun.

Video Games Forum (VIDEO GAMES)

Your kids can come into this forum for news and reviews of the hottest video games. More than any-thing, your kids will want to come here to exchange codes for their video games with other players. The message boards are full of requests for these codes and responses to these requests. Your kids can also search the libraries for files of codes and game-playing tips for every kind of video game you can think of. This is sure to be a favorite stop for your video gamer!

Dr. Gamewiz (GAMEWIZ)

Dr. Gamewiz is really Tom McConville, a self-pro-claimed professional game player. His role on America Online is personal game counselor to America Online's subscribers (see Figure 14.3). He will take your kids, step-by-step, through their favorite video games, unlocking secrets and sharing all of the hidden goodies of the game. These journeys take the form of walkthrough files and they literally take your

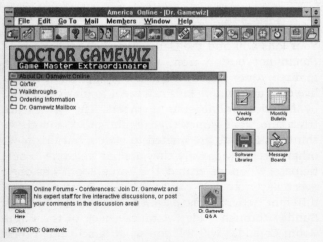

Figure 14.3 Dr. Gamewiz on America Online

kids on a walkthrough of their favorite video games to learn all of the insider tips and secrets! Your kids can read Dr. Gamewiz's weekly column, or go onto the message boards and ask him for help with their video games.

Online Gaming Forums (GAMING)

By entering the keyword, GAMING, your kids can pull up a menu of all of the gaming forums on America Online. These include the Role Playing Gaming Forum, the PC Games Forum, the Play-By-Mail Forum, the Strategy Forum, and forums dedicated to game designers and manufacturers. Bring her by this menu and explore some of these gaming options together.

COMPUSERVE

If you know the name of the game you want, and it's IBM- or Windows-based, use the PC File Finder (IBMFF). When we checked in, there were nearly 180,000 files of all types available.

We usually search by keyword. In our example, we looked for Commander Keen. Enter Keen, and instantly we're presented with a menu of files. Display the titles, and select the one you want. Then, download it by simply clicking on the hot button that says Retrieve. If you're interested in games for your Macintosh, use the Mac File Finder (MACFF). Select and retrieve from the more than 35,000 files here just as you did the IBM files.

If you don't know exactly which game you want, visit the gaming forums such as the Windows Fun forum. You can also get shareware, including games, from one of CompuServe's many forums. Use the find command and search under games to locate these forums.

Game Forums and News (GAMECON)

Bring your kids here and show them a menu for finding all of the major game-playing forums on

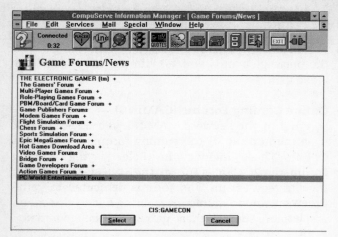

Figure 14.4 Game Forums and News on CompuServe

CompuServe (see Figure 14.4). This is a great place to get started. They can click on any one of the menu's entries to go right to the forum they want to explore.

- Action Games Forum (ACTION)
- CDROM Forum
- Epic MegaGames Forum
- Gamers Forum
- Mac Entertainment Forum
- Modem Games Forum
- Sega Forum
- Video Games Forum

Hot Games Download Area (HOTGAMES)

This is a convenient spot for checking out the latest games on CompuServe. When your child goes to Hot Games, she'll find a list of current titles for downloading. The games are stored here with complete instructions for downloading them, including the estimated download time and the equipment necessary for running the game. Games that start out in this area of CompuServe are later moved to their cor-

responding game forum, as new hot titles take their
places. The games are either shareware or demon-
stration versions of commercial programs.

Windows Fun Forum (WINFUN)
The libraries in this forum contain many games categorized by sections, such as card games, word games,
and action/adventure games. There's also a library
section named Just for Kids.

The Electronic Gamer ™ Archives (TEG—1)
Here your child will find copyrighted articles of
reviews and walkthroughs for popular games. The
articles are available only for their personal enjoyment, and may not be distributed, posted, or printed
anywhere else. The walkthroughs give complete solutions to the game, but the solutions are only one
person's way to complete the game. You may find your
own way that is different from what you read here.

Entertainment Center (ECENTER)
Those with IBM compatible computers can gather to
play live interactive games. Your kids can choose from
outer space type games or board games. Although
there is no additional fee for joining the Entertainment Center, online costs can add up quickly here.
Members can choose to join a pricing plan to control
costs. One such plan includes a monthly sign-up fee,
currently $10, and an hourly charge of $2.50. Check
the menu for the latest pricing information before
you decide if your kids should play.

PRODIGY

If you're going to download game software from
Prodigy, first you'll have to subscribe to another service, 2D Net Shareware Club. The cost is $3.50 per
month. You may use allotted time from your Prodigy
Plan toward your time spent in 2D Net. Additional
hours are billed at $2.95/hour. To access 2D Net, you

must have a DOS-based PC with 640K of RAM and a hard disk.

Prodigy offers a lot of games that your kids can play while they're online. The games described below are all included in Prodigy's core pricing package. We only described the ones we thought your kids might like to try. Your kids will find all of these games by clicking on the Games button you see on the Kids screen. Then, choose *Quick Games* to see the following games listed.

AJ Dakota & the Orb of Kings

This is a grid-based game that is popular and familiar to computer gamers (see Figure 14.5). It is set in a jungle adventure. You are expected to work your way through a "room" from the bottom left corner to the top left. Each square you step on will reveal the number of surrounding squares that are booby trapped. You get two chances to step on a booby-trapped square before you lose the game. It's a puzzling challenge.

Figure 14.5 AJ Dakota and the Orb of Kings on Prodigy

Boxes

A quick and easy game to play against a friend or the computer, this is what we called Othello in the days of board games. One player controls the white playing pieces, the other controls the black ones. Players take turns flipping each other's game pieces from white to black. The one with the most game pieces at the end (in our case, the computer), is the winner.

FITB

FITB (pronounced Fit-bee) means Fill in the Blanks. Up to four players can play to complete five words that appear on the screen. These five words will come together to give you the hints you need to guess the computer's secret word. Our category was "pickles." Our hints were "good on a hamburger" and "dill." Based on solving these two hints, and the number of letters in the category, we figured the computer must be looking for "pickles." Now, really, you must be impressed with our reasoning skills!

GUTS

This is an ongoing game that lasts for seven weeks. Each week, your kids have a total of seven minutes to answer up to seven trivia questions. Each week the questions get to be more difficult, and the scores for correctly answering the questions increase. At the end of seven weeks, one winner will have a biography placed in the winner's section. The top seven scorers will have their names posted, and they will also receive GUTS sweatshirts. You are billed for the seven minutes of connect time your child uses to answer the questions each week.

Police Artist

This is a face matching game. Prodigy shows you a villain (see Figure 14.6). After studying the face, you go on to choose, from menus, until you believe you've recreated the face exactly. The good news is,

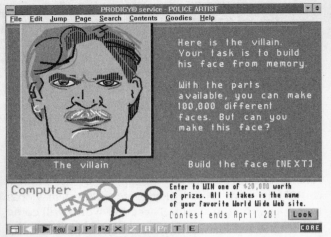

Figure 14.6 Police Artist on Prodigy

it's kind of cool. The bad news is that the variations of the facial features are so slight that even after you're sure you've done it right—I mean really sure, because you're good at this, you've done it again and again, and you're sure you're right—that computer will find something slightly off, and you'll be frustrated again.

Thinker

We call this Cows and Bulls. It's a guessing game that requires you to identify the digits of a three-digit number by using reasoning skills. We play it with a piece of paper and a pencil. It's every bit as challenging that way and just as much fun to play.

Square Off

You can only play this game once a day, and that is to Prodigy's credit. If your kids want to give it a try, they will probably use about 10 to 15 minutes of online time. The game includes two parts. During the first part, you get target numbers, and you must form equations that equal those numbers. The second part of the game gives you the equations, and you must add the operators (+ or -) to make the equation come out. Your score puts you in competition with others who play the game for the high-score list.

Carmen Sandiego

Moving down to the Humor/Fun hot button on the Games menu, you'll find Carmen Sandiego. If you love the show and the software, you'll want to love this online version of the game, but we don't think you will. It is a little too slow and too heavy in the text for it to seem like too much fun to us. No matter how many times we played, the game frustrated us by not being flexible enough in letting you move from clue to clue or from place to place. We're going to save our online time and spend the money on the CD-ROM instead.

Computer Gaming World

This is a selection under the *Game Hints* hot button. It is an online magazine for gamers. Your kids can find reviews and descriptions of new games in this area. They can also search the archives to get reviews of games that have been published in back issues.

This is another source of codes for Nintendo and Sega game systems. Computer Gaming World's hints are divided into two categories, Adventure/Role Playing Games and Strategy/Sports Games. Each month, your kids will find two new files added, usually one in each category. Game Hints also includes walkthroughs of popular games.

Game Poll

The Game Poll area allows you to rate up to thirty games each week. Rated from 1 to 10, you can vote on any game you've played or watched someone else play often enough to understand it. You can also read the results of the polls to see what the top-ranking games are. The polls run from Friday to Thursday, and new poll results are available after 6 P.M. on Fridays.

Games BB

The last hot button on the Games menu takes you to the Games BB and the Video Games BB.

The Games BB is for every kind of nonvideo game you can think of. Here you will find people pursuing all sorts of games, but keep in mind, this board is not meant for kids alone. Unless your child pursues a particular game, there are better places online for her to gather with friends and chat.

The Video Games BB is where your kids will want to be. This message board is filled with the latest in both home and arcade video game news and tips. Maybe the most important element in this message board are the game codes that visitors share. You can scan the board for help in obtaining codes to just about any video game. This is a hugely popular feature, and one to make your video gamer wild.

THE INTERNET

The World Wide Web

Help your kids get on the Internet and get their favorite games. Now. Never before has it been so easy to acquire this kind of great entertainment. The world's best game shareware and freeware, along with tips from the masters, are all waiting for you and yours on the net.

The Games Domain
(http://wcl-rs.bham.ac.uk/~-djh/index.html)
This is the spot on the net for all your game needs. Designed to be as simple to use as possible, the main area your kids will want to explore is the Direct Download section (see Figure 14.7). This offers easy access to hundreds of shareware games and demos from around the Internet. In the works when we checked were a Games Review and Games Programming section.

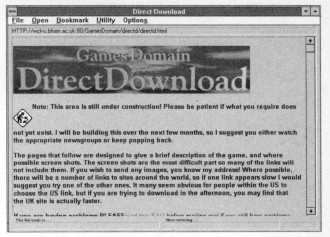

Figure 14.7 The Direct Download Page from the Games Domain
WWW Site

In addition to The Games Domain, your child can also retrieve games from a number of archives via "FTP." This process is a bit more complicated than getting games via the Web, but we did want to mention it is possible. FTP (File Transfer Protocol) is simply the process by which you transfer, or download, a file from the Internet to your own computer. Your Internet service provider or the commercial online service you use for Internet access, can tell you how FTP operates on the service you use.

THE BEST GAMES FOR KIDS ON THE NET

Dave Stanworth, a 28-year-old computer programmer working at the University of Birmingham, runs The Games Domain, the most popular games site on the WWW.

(More than 2 million requests during a typical month!)

Here's his personal list of the top games for PCs on the Net. They are all available from The Game Domain's

"Direct Download" section. We've also included the FTP (file transfer protocol) instructions in case there are net savants out there who want to go that route.

Most games are also available from the commercial online services.

1. Jazz Jackrabbit
   Look out Sonic. Jazz Jackrabbit is coming toward you at light speed, and this little bunny carries a big gun! Lead the animated Jazz across the galaxy to save kidnapped bunny princess Eva Earlong.
   Age: 8–Adult
   Publisher: Epic MegaGames
   FTP: ftp.uml.edu/msdos/Games/Epic/1jazz.zip
   Size: 1390Kb

2. One Must Fall 2097
   Welcome to the future of fighting from Epic MegaGames. In the year 2097 steel will bend and sparks will fly. You control a massive robot through match after match of strategic fighting action. The best fighting game available that concentrates on game play and not on violence.
   Age: 8–Adult
   Publisher: Epic MegaGames
   FTP: ftp.uml.edu/msdos/Games/Epic/1omf2097.zip
   Size: 2677Kb

3. Wacky Wheels
   A high-speed, VGA 3D point-of-view, full screen racing game. The shareware version has 5 race tracks plus specialty tracks for shoot outs. Also, it has a two-player mode via split screen at same PC, or via modem or serial cable. Many options & features. Excellent cartoon graphics.
   Age: 8–Adult
   Publisher: Apogee
   FTP: ftp.uml.edu/msdos/Games/Apogee/1wacky.zip
   Size: 1625Kb

4. Math Rescue
   A funny adventure-filled Nintendo-style EGA/VGA multi-scrolling learning game. Includes puzzling

Kidnet

word/math problems and arithmetic.
Age: 5–14
Publisher: Apogee
FTP: ftp.uml.edu/msdos/Games/Apogee/1math.zip
Size: 419Kb

5. Word Rescue
Educational game for children, yet a great challenge for adults, too. Tons of colorful and elaborate graphics. Play as a male or a female character and explore many fascinating locations as you search for all the stolen words. Three difficulty levels.
Age: 5–14
Publisher: Apogee
FTP: ftp.uml.edu/msdos/Games/Apogee/1rescue.zip
Size: 368Kb

6. Cosmo's Cosmic Adventure
Full-screen wide adventure/action platform game. Show-stopping animation! Help Cosmo rescue his parents on a peril-packed planet! Three difficulty levels.
Age: 8–Adult
Publisher: Apogee
FTP: ftp.uml.edu/msdos/Games/Apogee/1cosmo.zip
Size: 512Kb

7. Adventure Math
An excellent shareware learning experience. Solve addition & subtraction problems in 256 snazzy VGA colors. Makes learning fun.
Age: 5–10
Publisher: Epic MegaGames
FTP: ftp.uml.edu/msdos/Games/Epic/amath.zip
Size: 369Kb

8. Heartlight
Guide the elf Percival through twenty levels of puzzles featuring 256-color animated graphics! Heartlight is a puzzle game, and you'll get hooked as you try to conquer all its ingenious levels.
Age: 10–Adult
Publisher: Epic MegaGames

FTP: ftp.uml.edu/msdos/Games/Epic/heart.zip
Size: 550Kb

9. Shooting Gallery
   Test your reflexes and hand/eye coordination with target shooting. All the fun of the fair and excellent for teaching someone how to use a computer mouse.
   Age: 8–Adult
   FTP: ftp.uml.edu/msdos/Games/Misc/shot23.zip
   Size: 94Kb

10. Elfland
    In Elfland, you "become" either Elfie (the male elf) or Elfita (the female elf). As you work your way through Elfland, you'll encounter obstacles, creatures of all stripes, and hazards. There's also plenty of music and sound effects to keep you going!

Michel Buffa's Video Games Page
(http://www.cs.cmu.edu/afs/cs.cmu.edu/user/buffa/www/videogames.html)

Updated daily, this is the best site for video game fans. Whether your child is into Sega, Game Boy, 3DO, or even old fashioned pinball, there are links and resources galore here. Press releases about enhancements, game specs, interviews with gaming illuminaries, and all manner of FAQs are here.

Zarf's List of Interactive Games on the WEB
(http://www.cs.cnu.edu:8001/afs/cs.cmu.edu/user/zarf/www/games.html)

A well maintained site broken down into two areas: Interactive games covering multiplayer games, you against the computer games, adventure games, and "anything else which sounds like a game;" and Interactive Toys. (According to the Webmaster these are "things that you can fool around with, that don't necessarily have a real goal.") Your child can play the interactive games right online, including some that are vocabulary-building.

Sega Web
(http://www.segaoa.com/)
Sega fans won't want to miss this site, which includes news and events areas, games hints (by platform), and audio/video clips. It's sort of a mega advertisement, but your kids won't care.

Play by Mail Games Homepage (T)
(http://fermi.clas.virginia.edu/~-gl8f/pbm.html)
This site includes lists of all known Play by Mail email and snail mail games. There are links to some of the more popular PBM games. There's an FAQ here to get you up to speed on this whole phenomenon. This area is for older kids only, as these games are usually rather involved.

The Pinball Pasture
(http://www.lysator.liu.se/pinball/)
"Dedicated to pinball and nothing but pinball."
It includes a showroom where popular games are described and shown.

Newsgroups and Mailing Lists

There are more than 130 newsgroups and 40 mailing lists devoted to games. Perhaps it's best if your child sticks to playing games rather than also reading and receiving mail about them. You know what they say about too much of a good thing.

THE BEST OF THE REST

eWorld

BMUG's User Group Forum (BMUG)
The Berkeley Macintosh User's Group is the biggest group of its type. As part of their charter, they've gathered an impressive collection of Macintosh shareware. You'll find some of it here, just click on the BMUG Shareware Library icon. When we did, we found a folder for education, but your kids will be glad to know we also found one for entertainment.

Retrieving the software is easy. Just click on the *Get File Now* icon. You're prompted for a file destination; after you respond, the download begins.

The Best of BMUG folder includes some games, such as Klondike (a classic solitaire game), but they're mixed in with other types of software programs such as utilities. Subfolders for software types would have made navigating this folder easier.

Software Center (SHAREWARE)

Here's a much more active, fuller, and better organized place to get games for your kids. When your kids click on *Software Central*, then *Games*, they'll find plenty of shareware. You'll find categories for adventure and arcade games, childrens games, strategy and card games, and game tips and tricks.

The ImagiNation Network

The ImagiNation Network is an online gamer's dream come true! It's colorful, musical, lively, and fun. Everything about this service is graphic, even the log-on procedure. While your modem dials out, you get to watch a little signal travel from your house, via satellite, to the ImagiNation Network. Sometimes a friendly dinosaur watches, too.

Once online, the service is set up to be visual and easy to use. The main screen is a map of a lively land. Click on the buildings to move from place to place.

If you decide to join the ImagiNation Network, you'll use the service's email and live chat features. The difference between using these features here and using them on other online services, is that here your only goal will be to visit with the gaming friends you'll meet. People on the ImagiNation are here for the fun of it!

As we told you in Chapter 1, before you log onto the ImagiNation Network, you create a little image of yourself that becomes your icon. The other people online will view you this way. You can also list some information about yourself. You can list up to four

Figure 14.8 The ImagiNation Network Waiting Room in the Clubhouse

hobbies, and rate your experience level for each of the games

Once online, choose the area you want to visit, for example, SierraLand. Your first stop will be the waiting room where other gamers gather. Figure 14.8 shows you the type of screen you'll see in the waiting room. As you can see, you can look at the icons of any of the gamers, and you can invite anyone to play with you. You can also choose to just watch a game if you'd like. If you get invited to play a game, and you don't know how, don't be bashful. Just ask for some directions and jump right in.

SierraLand

SierraLand is the area for arcade-style games, board games, and games that test your math and art talents. When we stopped into SierraLand, we found lots of kids playing. We'll describe a few of your choices here.

Red Baron

When we were in the waiting room, we received an invitation to play Red Baron. We're so glad we did! It's a lively World War 1 dogfight. We flew the plane, tried to find the enemy, and got killed in action. The game was fast, the graphics exciting, and the opponent nice enough to say we didn't do too badly for first timers!

Boogers

What kid could resist a game named Boogers? No one in our family. Boogers is a territorial game played with gloppy looking playing pieces. Take at look at Figure 14.9, and you'll see what we mean. Kids take turns trying to turn their opponents' playing pieces into their own color. The one who captures the most territory by the end of the game is the winner. When we watched, a 10-year-old girl was womping a 24-year-old man! Up to four people can play at once.

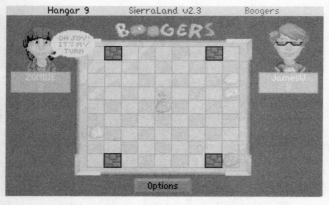

Figure 14.9 Boogers in Play on the ImagiNation Network

Sneak-A-Tac

This is an animated version of 3D tic-tac-toe. The board is 4 layers of grids that each have 16 squares. You can look at Figure 14.10 to get the idea. The object of the game is to be the first person to connect 4 boxes vertically, horizontally, or diagonally on a single level or on spanning levels. Sneak-A-Tac is not easy to play. It forces you to think about the game strategy in 3D terms.

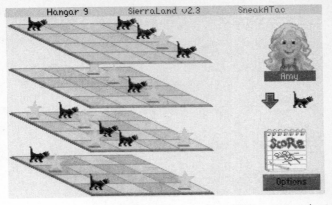

Figure 14.10 Sneak-A-Tac in Play on the ImagiNation Network

The Little Red Funhouse

By the time you read this, the ImagiNation Network expects to have a new version of its software available. This will include the Little Red Funhouse, an educational game center designed especially for kids ages 7 through 12. We weren't able to play any of the games that will be in this area, but based on the other areas we saw, they should be lively and fun.

The Town Hall

This is the place to stop for help in using the service or to ask questions about your account. Look for people with INN in their names. These are staff members who will gladly show you around and help you learn to play any of the games you may want to try.

Appendix A

Basic System Commands
for the Three Major Commercial
Online Services

America Online
Navigation Command
- Ctrl-K for "Keyword"

Main Menu
- Ctrl-D for "Departments"

Mail
- Use the pull-down menu or enter Ctrl-M for writing mail and Ctrl-R for reading it.

Keyword List
- Ctrl-K to get the Keyword dialog box. Click on Keyword List button.

Interrupt
- Hit the Escape key to stop a command already in progress

Log Off
- Pull down the File menu, highlight Exit and click

CompuServe
Navigation Command
- Ctrl G for "Go"

Main Menu
- Enter TOP

Mail
- GO MAIL

Go Word List
- GO INDEX

Interrupt
- Ctrl C, enter once or maybe twice

Log Off
- Pull down the File menu or click on the Disconnect icon.

Prodigy
Navigation Command
- Ctrl J for "Jump"

Main Menu
- Jump HIGHLIGHTS

Mail
- JUMP MAIL

Jump Word List
- Click on "A-Z" tool at the bottom of the screen

Log Off
- Click on the "E" tool at the bottom of the screen or pull down the file menu.

Appendix B

Electronic Bulletin Boards and Free-Nets

There are ways you can go online without accessing the Internet or the commercial online services we've covered in this book. Going online doesn't have to cost a lot of money, or any money at all. Read on.

Bulletin Boards

There's a nationwide network of thousands of free or almost free dial-up online services. They may not be as well known as Prodigy or America Online, but millions of people use them. Commonly known as Bulletin Board Systems (BBSs for short), there are tens of thousands of such boards. Most are run by hobbyists. They are an excellent place to get your online sea legs, and to download software, too.

BBSs typically offer software, message boards, news—in short, much of what their larger counterparts offer. Some provide free access; most charge a fee ranging from $25 to $99 per year. As you might imagine, kids (and adults) mostly access boards in order to download software. A few boards offer access to the Internet, but this is far from the norm.

Naturally, we recommend that kids stick to boards geared toward them. Unfortunately, these are rare, so to use BBSs, you may need to cast a wider net. Be watchful of which BBSs your child is using. You'll find, for example, that a few boards specialize in nude image files. These usually charge closer to the $99 end of the price range cited above, which is enough to deter most kids.

To find out if there are local bulletin boards in your area, contact a local computer store. If they can't help you, they may distribute local computer newsletters (which typically list numbers for boards), or be able to put you in touch with your local computer users group. Once you get on a BBS, it's easy to track down other boards; most contain lists of other BBSs.

Commercial services may also be of help. America Online, for example, has an entire section devoted to bulletin board systems. The keyword is BBS.

Boardwatch magazine, at the time of this writing, planned to start a monthly column about BBSs and kids. Watch for it. For further information about *Boardwatch* magazine, call 800.933.6038.

Free-Nets

There are scores of free-nets across the U.S. and abroad. They are something of a cross between commercial online services and electronic bulletin boards. Unlike BBSs, free-nets are organized and run by communities, rather than individuals. They are nonprofit and exist to make local information available to the community at large and for educational purposes in general. The best part about free-nets is that it costs little to access them—$10–$25 per year is the norm.

You access a free-net by dialing (via modem, of course) a local number. You'll need to use a generic communications program, such as those described in Chapter 2. Actually, logging on and getting around free-nets may be somewhat more difficult than accessing a commercial service. They tend to have text-only interfaces, rather than the handsome graphical interfaces of commercial services. However, menus help new users feel comfortable on a free-net in very little time. Because they are often busy, you may sometimes have trouble logging onto your local free-net.

Many free-nets provide limited access to the Internet. This typically includes electronic mail, newsgroups, gopher sites and, in some cases, World Wide Web access.

Many free-nets also include "cybercasts" from the National Public Telecomputing Network (NPTN). These cybercasts may include information and communications features for grade school students, health information, and government information services.

A listing of free-nets is available from the National Public Telecomputing Network. Contact them at:

30680 Bainbridge Road
Solon, OH 44139
Voice: 216.498.4050
Fax: 216.498.4051
General email: info@nptn.org

Glossary

Access Number
A phone number, preferably local, you can use to dial into an online service.

Address
Online, as offline, this is the location at which people can reach you. Your address will be different on each service you join.

BPS
The acronym for bits per second. In modem language the speed at which information is transferred. The more bits, the better.

CD-ROM
Compact disk, read-only memory, a high capacity storage device. Information on the CD-ROM cannot be altered, only read. A CD-ROM holds the equivalent of hundreds of standard diskettes.

Communications Program
A type of software program that provides the instruction your computer needs to operate your modem.

Compress
Reduce a file's size to make transferring it less time consuming. Once a file is compressed, it's sort of like concentrated orange juice—minus the water. You "decompress" a file (add water) after you have retrieved it.

Download
To transfer a computer file, from a remote computer to your own.

Electronic Bulletin Boards

Informal online services, usually run by hobbyists. They are most commonly used for online communications and for downloading software.

Electronic Chat

A live conversation that takes place online. An electronic chat can happen between two people or in much larger groups. Large group chats are commonly called conferences. CB simulator is another term used for electronic chatting.

Electronic Mail

Mail that's exchanged between computer users.

Emoticons

Collections of keyboard characters used to express emotion in online communications :-). They are meant to be read with your head tipped slightly to the left.

FAQ (Frequently Asked Questions)

Commonly posted to Internet newsgroups, these set the ground rules for the newsgroup's use, and answer the most common questions. It's good manners to read these before posting to a newsgroup.

Flame

An insult delivered online, usually via email.

Forum

An online gathering place for people who share common interests.

Free-Net

Sort of a cross between a commercial online service and an electronic bulletin board, Free-Nets are community-based online information services.

FTP
File Transfer Protocol. This defines how files are
retrieved via the Internet.

GIF
See Graphics Files.

Gopher Site
On the Internet, a place from which you can retrieve
files. A menuing system makes sifting through the
files simple.

Graphics Files
Electronic versions of photographs, works of art, or
other images. These are usually larger (sometimes a
lot larger) than files consisting of text only. But they
do compress well. Popular formats for files include
.GIF (the standard on CompuServe) and .JPEG.

Hypertext
A navigational aid popular on the Internet's World
Wide Web. In a hypertext document, if you click on a
word that's highlighted you'll jump automatically to
a related document. In this way, everything on the
World Wide Web is linked.

Icon
A graphic that represents a choice of action. For
example, by clicking on a small picture of a printer,
you can print the information that is currently on
your screen.

Interface
The face the online service shows the world. Graphical User Interfaces (GUIs) are the easiest to use.

Internet Relay Chat (IRC)
The Internet's version of the electronic chat or CB services that are so popular on the commercial services.

Internet Service Provider (ISP)

A company that provides people with access to the Internet. ISPs usually provide you with a suite of software tools to use with their service (see Shareware). Some ISPs furnish proprietary software meant for use only with their services.

ISDN

Integrated Services Digital Network, a standard for sending voice, video, and data over communications lines. ISDN services, becoming more widely available, allow online communication at rates several times faster than what is currently possible with today's fastest modems and standard telephone lines.

JPEG

See Graphics Files.

Keypal

A pen pal you communicate with via email.

Lurking

Observing an online activity without participating. The term is often used in conjunction with message boards and live chats.

Mailing List

On the Internet, mailing lists are like newsgroups, except the communication is usually one-way. People who belong to mailing lists share a common interest. Postings are automatically sent to everyone who has subscribed to the mailing list.

Message Thread

Online message responses, usually posted on forums, that all relate to one original posting and therefore share a common topic.

Modem
A device that allows computers to communicate via telephone lines.

Mouse
A computer device that allows you to control the movement of the cursor on your computer screen. A mouse makes it possible for you to control the cursor simply by pointing and clicking a button.

Netiquette
The rules for polite behavior in the online society.

Network
Computers that are linked together for the purpose of sharing information.

Newsgroups
On the Internet, electronic bulletin boards dedicated to particular topics. The 10,000 Newsgroups now on the Internet are collectively known as Usenet.

Online
The condition that exists when one computer is connected to another computer, usually via a telephone line.

Online Service
A company that provides computer access via modem, to information and software.

Password
Your unique identifier that insures the security of your online account.

PPP
Point-to-Point Protocol, a way to connect to other computers via the telephone line.

PKZIP
The most popular file compression program in the IBM world. Files compressed with PKZIP have the extension .zip.

Shareware
Software made available on a try-before-you-buy basis. It is often available for downloading through commercial online services, the Internet, and electronic bulletin boards. If you like it, you are obligated to pay the software author the registration fee.

SLIP
Serial Line Internet Protocol, a method of connecting your computer to the Internet via your telephone line.

Spoiler
A warning in a message that plot details (often of a movie) are included in the posting.

Sysop
A member of the administrative staff responsible for maintaining a particular online area.

Upload
Send a file from your computer to another one.

Uniform Resource Listing (URL)
A standard that applies to addressing Web sites such as HTTP://whitehouse.gov.

Usenet
An umbrella term for all of the Internet's newsgroups.

Webmaster
The sysop behind a Web site charged with maintaining and updating the site. See the World Wide Web listing below.

Windows 95
The latest version (after 3.1) of Microsoft's popular Windows operating system.

World Wide Web (WWW)
A part of the Internet, now consisting of more than 40,000 multimedia-rich "sites," each devoted to a particular company, person, or topic. Hyperlinking makes it easy to bounce from one WWW site to another.

Index

Index

Index

285

Index